THE

WHISPERED

WORD

THE
WHISPERED
WORD

A THEOLOGY OF PREACHING

MARJORIE
HEWITT
SUCHOCKI

Chalice Press
St. Louis, Missouri

Cover Photograph: Lorrie Calabrese Keller
Cover Design: Arista Graphics
Art Director: Elizabeth Wright
Interior Design: Wynn Younker

This book is printed on acid-free, recycled paper.

Visit Chalice Press on the World Wide Web at
www.chalicepress.com

10 9 8 7 6 5 4 3 2 1   99 00 01 02 03 04

Library of Congress Cataloging–in–Publication Data

Suchocki, Marjorie.
    The whispered word: a theology of preaching / by Marjorie Hewitt Suchocki.
        p.   cm
    ISBN 0-8272-4239-5
    1. Preaching.   I. Title
    BV4211.2.S87   1999   99-21271
    251—dc21   CIP

Printed in the United States of America

*This book is gratefully dedicated
to my students
at Claremont School of Theology
and Northwest House of Theological Studies*

Acknowledgments

The Three Rivers Annual Conference (Illinois) of The United Methodist Church graciously invited me to give a series of five lectures to its pastors on a theology of preaching. Those five lectures became the basis of this book, and I am grateful to the Annual Conference for the challenge to think in these directions.

I also thank three of my colleagues at Claremont School of Theology for their generous help as I ventured into the "far country" of their own areas of expertise: Prof. Kathy Black, Gerald Kennedy Associate Professor of Preaching and Worship; Prof. Joseph Webb, Associate Professor of Homiletics; and Prof. Jack Coogan, Professor of Communication Arts. Thanks also to my colleague A. J. Levine, Carpenter Professor of New Testament Studies at Vanderbilt Divinity School, for her help with Chapter 4.

My thanks also go to Dr. David Polk of Chalice Press, who encouraged me to turn the lectures into this book, and named it *The Whispered Word*.

Contents

1

The Whispered Word

There is an ancient tale told by Augustine that sets the context for developing a process theology of preaching.[1] Augustine, you will remember, pondered the dilemma of how so perfect a creature as Adam, brought into being directly from the hand and breath of God, could sin. His resolution to the problem forced him away from the human scene to a drama in heaven long before human creatures took form. God had made the angels, many and various, greatly beautiful, utterly wonderful—and yet, creatures, made out of nothingness, even as would be the earth and its life in the time to come. This "out-of-nothingness" quality is what separated these creatures from God, for whereas God's own being was underived, springing up eternally, the immortal angels had a derived life. They depended continuously upon their source of life, God. The work of these glorious creatures was to enjoy God and to praise God forever.

So far in the story, so good. But as Augustine saw it, the crack in the golden bowl came at just this point. Think of it: If you were an angel, created with a derived immortality, whose work and whose bliss was to enjoy and praise God forever, wouldn't it occur to you that your continuation in this state really depended on God's good pleasure? This immortality you enjoyed was in fact a gift—what if the giver took it back? If you were a supremely intelligent angel, with all eternity encompassing you, wouldn't you sooner or later have the passing thought that your existence was, after all, a bit contingent? Only God has necessary existence, not angels!

So perhaps, in this eternal contemplation of yours, you might occasionally wonder if you could really *count* on this God to continue to sustain you! But alas, if this piece of doubt entered your head, why then, you wouldn't be trusting God, would you? And if you weren't really trusting God, then your enjoyment and praise would be a bit deficient, and you would find yourself a fallen angel on the spot!

Actually, of course, Augustine could count on an omniscient God to have foreseen the problem. It would never do for all the heavenly host at some point in eternity to worry and fall—and indeed, once the first one fell, all the others would certainly have cause for alarm, which by definition in this particular story would be already to have fallen. So God built a resolution into the system. God spoke a word into the ears of a certain number of the angels assuring them that they would never fall, that they would continue forever in their infinite bliss. And knowing full well that God's word cannot fail, these angels could be stalwart and persevering in the grace of that word, no matter how many other angelic beings bit the dust, so to speak.

The point of the story is that the word of God saves by engendering the trust that is itself salvation, but that this word is spoken only to some, not to all. And therein lies the tragedy. Those angels who heard no word of grace assuring them that they should persevere turned from the praise of God to doubt their own ability to continue in that praise. And alas, the turn from God to self, whether angelic or otherwise, is the beginning of sin and damnation in the Augustinian universe. Our very life depends upon our being hearers of the Word.

In a process world there is indeed agreement on this point: Our very lives depend upon our being hearers of God's word. But a process perspective takes this even further, claiming that there is not only no life, but no creaturely existence at all apart from the continuously creative word of God. For complex creatures such as ourselves and angels—if angels there be—God's creative word inaugurates and supports every microscopic millisecond of our lives. The Genesis description of God's creative activity as issuing from a word ("And

God *said…!"*) describes not simply a once-long-ago creative work of God, but God's ongoing work of creation as well. God's manner of creation is in and through a word. Process theology suggests that God is everlastingly creative, continuously calling existence into being through an evocative word. To put it another way, God is Creator not because once God created and that was that, but because the everlasting God is everlastingly Creator, and that the way of this divine creation is through a word. Even as we speak, God is calling all worlds, and thus even our world, and ourselves with it, into being.

God's given word is not limited to humanity, nor do we who delve in process thought (alas) even call this creative gift of God a "word": We instead say, "initial aim," such as: "Every occasion of existence begins with an initial aim from God that guides the becoming occasion toward what it might yet be!" What is meant by this somewhat infelicitous way of putting it is that nothing—absolutely nothing—could exist apart from God's word directed toward each bit of newly becoming stuff. Everything that exists does so because it has received and responded, to some extent, to a word specifically directed to it by God. Thus, a process version of the Augustinian story would have to assert that God could not have withheld a word from even one angel, for had God withheld a word, the angel would have ceased to exist. To exist is, by definition, to be receiving a word from God.

But of course there's more to it than that, as was indicated by my slightly qualifying phrase, "to some extent," relative to the occasion's response to God. For in this process world, God's creative word is given as invitation and as promise. As promise, it suggests that which is truly possible for the emerging reality; as invitation, it calls that reality toward precisely this invited becoming. But an invitation, no matter how promising, calls for a response, and therein lies the freedom of the world—and with that freedom, the greatness and the tragedy of the world. God calls: We answer. In the answering we participate along with God in our own ongoing creation. Responding, we are responsible.

We will deal further with this responsibility later; for now, we focus still more strongly on this creative word of God.

The process phrase "initial aim" suggests that God's creative word launches us anew in every moment of our existence, initiating the directive energy that aims us toward what we might become. This word is felt within the depths of the self, which suggests that God's word comes to us as a whisper. It is not loud, like a clanging symbol, nor is it boisterous, calling attention to itself and insisting on its own program. To the contrary, it is a quiet word, a suggestive word, an inviting word, not always easily noticed. How awesome that the word of the living God should come to us quietly, like a whisper. But process thought suggests that this is the case, and for at least four reasons.

First, God's word to every existent becoming thing—whether animal, vegetable, or mineral—is contextual. God's word does not ignore us and our circumstances, speaking imperiously as if none of that mattered. Rather, our peculiarities of time and personality and space do indeed matter, for God's word to us encounters the realities of our distant and immediate past with the possibilities of what our immediate and distant future might yet be. God's creative word meets our condition, emerging quietly and most often unnoticeably in the midst of who and where we are. Precisely because God's word takes full account of our circumstances, it is a redemptive word—for only a God who knows us more thoroughly than we know ourselves knows what is really possible for us given our situation.

Let me situate this for us through an illustration. David loves his wife, but she left him and served divorce papers during the holidays. Clearly, David is very troubled. But complicating his situation is the fact that he and his wife recently moved to California in order to make an important change in his career that would allow him the opportunity to enroll in M.Div. studies at Claremont School of Theology. While his studies are working out well, his new part-time career is not, and it is doubtful whether or not he will be able to sustain his position and, therefore, his financial viability. In other words, I want you to picture a person who is most certainly involved in a mid-life crisis of awesome proportions. His personal and professional life is in chaos. I have said that

God gives a creative word in every moment—but before you ask what kind of a creative word got David into such a fix, fix your attention on the challenges of getting him out of it. How is God to address him? If God worked independently of his situation, overriding his circumstances, how could this help David deal with precisely this mess? Wouldn't God be providing yet one more opportunity for gross failure? Rather, God continuously enters into David's situation, knowing it more thoroughly than David does himself. God does indeed transcend the world, but God is also in the midst of things, incarnate in our worlds, a God of presence. God knows David's situation.

Precisely because God knows David so well, God knows the steps that can lead him from despair to deliverance, from these little deaths to resurrection. But the transformative steps are accomplished incrementally—bit by bit, step by step. Call and response, call and response, call and response: Over and over and over God makes possible a reality-based way of dealing with the situation, no matter how difficult it is. Womanist theologians have taught me the phrase "God makes a way out of no way." It aptly describes the deeply contextual work of God.

Each word of God to David reflects possibilities that are compatible with David's particular past and can lead him to a new future. David's responsiveness to each word makes way for the next word. Transformation will occur through God's faithfulness and David's responsiveness. There is no situation, no matter how dreadful, beyond the creative and transformative power of God. The word of God is incarnational, clothed in the flesh of the past, but offering the possibility of a new future.

But notice the peculiarity. Because God works incarnationally, God's word weaves the past together in fresh and redemptive ways moment by moment. This is both the power of God and the hiddenness of God. The power rests in the accessibility of the transformation God offers. The hiddenness rests in its mundane quality: It is most often a baby step, not a giant step, and it can emerge as a very ordinary thing. Who would think the transforming and creative word of God could appear as ordinary? And yet have you not seen it time and time again? The Davids who come for pastoral counseling feel hopeless—yet they come for help, which is itself a sign of hope. Their progress seems slow to them and to the pastor. Yet they slowly integrate their losses into who they are; they can reckon with themselves as known and loved by God; they can move on to a deeper sensitivity. David may yet join the ranks of wounded healers, his arrogance worn away, and a new faithfulness born in him that is reflective of the faithfulness of God. Between now and then there is a patient working deep down: God calls and David responds, again and again and again.

Hence the whisper quality of God's creative word: It can easily be drowned out by the sheer weight of the past with which and through which it must work. It is clothed in the past even as it bespeaks a future, and it leads us not through extraordinary leaps and bounds, but most often through a quite ordinary faithfulness in the midst of things. God's word is hidden incarnationally in the world. It is a whisper.

Second, God's creative word is a whisper simply through its habituation. There is never a moment when God does *not* offer a formative word. One seldom notices one's heart beat simply because it is always there: One likewise can live in the constancy of God's guiding word without particular notice. There is an awesomeness to this aspect of God's word. How can it be that the God of the universe should be so taken for granted? All of our notions of honor and privilege are turned upside down by such a God. It appears that it is we, not God, who place such importance on rank and power. We assign special seating according to one's rank in society; we take particular care with those we name VIPs (as if all persons were not Very Important!); we revere the rich and famous.

And all the while the God of the universe whose creative word has spun the stars and galaxies into space works quietly in ways almost unnoticed among and through us. Oh, we call attention to God's glory in our hymns and prayers of a Sunday morning—but could it be the case that it is we, not God, who need all these thoughts of glory? Perhaps the glory of God is the wondrous faithfulness of God, everlastingly creative, everlastingly redemptive, everlastingly sustaining, everlastingly present, holding the universe in being through a word hidden deep in the heart of each thing. And God's faithfulness is so constant that we take it for granted as the way things are.

The very constancy of God, then, can be like a veiling of God. We have no idea what it would be like to be without God because this is totally beyond our experience. So, then, if God's word comes to us as a whisper because of the incarnational quality of the word as it works with our past, God's word also comes as a whisper because we are so accustomed to it as part of the background of our lives.

Third, and perhaps most telling, the word is a whisper because of its depth dimension. Necessarily, the word is at the inauguration of each moment, in the very depths of the becoming process. The process parlance illumines the situation: God's word comes as an "initial aim." In Whitehead's model, consciousness is a late phase of each momentary being, but the initial aim is the beginning phase. The content of the aim provides direction for how we might become ourselves in each moment; it offers a possible integration of the past in light of a best future. By the time consciousness is achieved, the initial word has been transformed into a subjective word of one's own intent.

An illustration from teaching gives an analogy. Have you ever noticed, whether in a class or a committee, the peculiar dynamic when an idea you suggest is received by the group, worked on, developed, and brought to fruition? When the process works best, the idea finally becomes the group's own idea, with no particular remembrance of whence the idea first emerged. Even so with God's initial aim: The aim evokes the responsiveness of our own subjectivity, which adapts God's guiding word according to our own purposes. The process way of putting it is to say that God's initial aim becomes adapted to our own subjective aim, and in the process, the word from God is transformed for good or for ill into our own word.

We are accustomed in our day to the language of depth psychology that speaks to subconscious and unconscious aspects of the human psyche. Imagine this in a dynamic way. Imagine that every second is the recreation of consciousness, and that this happens initially through an unconscious grasping of all influences impinging upon us. There is much sorting and sifting even in this initial phase, which yields a more organized ordering of data in what could be called the subconscious aspect of our mentality. Here the various influences inherited from our world (including our body) are formed into constellations of events analogous to the archetypal world described by the psychologist Carl Jung. But not even this is consciousness—it is the doorway to consciousness, that which makes consciousness possible—and it is accessible to us in our dreams. Consciousness itself is the culminating phase of our mentality, and in some respects consciousness can be viewed as the final organization of data into meaning and action. It is that aspect of ourselves that we experience as decisive, as choosing, as thinking. But in the holistic reality and complexity of ourselves, it is a tip-of-the-iceberg sort of thing. We decide and choose and think, not in a vacuum, but through the supporting web of experience hovering at the edges of our consciousness.

Have you not noticed this in your own life? For me it often happens in the writing process. I always have a perfectly dreadful time in the first few days I devote to writing, for nothing at all is done! I set aside a block of time for writing, but on the first day I think of an errand I must do, or maybe I should clean the closet, or tend to a left-over detail from my administrative work. It doesn't matter what it is: It's just that it's guaranteed to be something, and it frustrates me no end. But at some point I finally figure it out. What's happening in this time is that somewhere deeper than my consciousness there is a sorting-out going on, a kind of sifting of things. The whole time that I am putting off writing, I am actually organizing the writing, so that when my consciousness finally tunes in, I'm ready. I make decisions about my writing before I know it.

Another illustration comes from those times when we are worrying about a problem for which we see no solution. "I'll sleep on it," we say, and the surprising thing is that when we wake up we really do see a solution. An aspect of our minds deeper than consciousness is doing the work. Our mentality is more than our consciousness, and our decision-making processes do not begin with consciousness, but culminate with consciousness. It's as if the cake is already made, but now we have to add the frosting.

Lest this sound like an overly rational account, let me hasten to add that emotional tone is highly important to the process, and much of the preconscious work deals with the raw emotional responses to whatever issues we face. Emotions provide a guiding impetus in the early organizing phases of this process. In a sense, feeling gives rise to thought.

What I am describing is like a cross-section of a process that dynamically repeats itself instant by instant, so rapidly that it gives the illusion of constant consciousness. In actuality, however, consciousness flickers in and out of existence—like those lines marking the different cells in an old motion picture film that totally disappear given the rapidity with which the film is run.

And what does this brief description of consciousness add to our understanding of God's creative word as being like a whisper? Since God's word begins each momentary existence of becoming, God's word comes at that unconscious or preconscious phase. This is part of the power of the word—it is given at the earliest stage in which experience is organized, giving direction at the very beginning. We grasp that word, using it as we deal with the barrage of data affecting us—but that we are doing so is not yet a part of our consciousness. By the subconscious level we have adapted God's word to our own situation; it now affects those swirling constellations that are like the organizing motifs of our being. And at the conscious level we are like that committee that has run with a suggestion, making it its own. The source is no longer in view.

Throughout this process some degree of autonomy—freedom—is operative. This is to say that responsibility is deeper than consciousness. God proposes. We dispose of that proposal for the good or ill of ourselves and others first of all at the unconscious level of our being. God's proposal is an invitation that can be rejected, accepted, or in some way adapted. So, then, the depth dimension of God's word as it comes to us, and our adaptation of that word into our own formed purposes, serve to render God's word a whisper, almost out of the range of our hearing. . . almost.

And finally, I often think the word is a whisper by God's own preferential design. The orientation of God's initial aim toward each one of us is toward our own communal good in this world. Only seldom does the gift of the initial aim call attention to the giver; most often, the gift launches us toward the world in concern for increasing parameters of well-being. Of course, since God feels the world, all things eventually return to God. But it seems to me that the content of God's word itself does not usually direct us back to God (although it can and sometimes does), but forward toward the world.

In a sense, this draws us into God's own creative work. It's as if God has created us not as individuals unto ourselves, but as participants in a world; we are created for one another. To this end, God works creatively deep within each one of us, but in such a way that our responsiveness to God is precisely to the extent that we act responsibly in the world toward our common good. It's as if God creates *within* the depths of each one of us, and also on the surface *through* each one of us.

Consider David again. God is working deep within him, but God is also working deep within his friends. His friends feel concern for David and reach out to him supportively. No doubt God, working within them, calls them to this ministry. But in this case, God is working on more than one level. God works directly with David in and through the initial aims continually given to him in the depths of his being. And God works indirectly with David in and through what his friends are doing with the aims God has given them. God works with us contextually, not only in the depths of ourselves, but also in and through community. As David's friends receive and respond to God's call, their thoughts are probably less toward the God who prompts them to this service and more toward their friend whose need is so apparent.

In caring for David, they are responding to God, even while, paradoxically, they may not notice that this in fact is what is happening. God has directed them not to Godself, but to David.

John Wesley has a wonderfully pertinent word concerning this in my favorite little book, *A Plain Account of Christian Perfection*. There he says on page 103 that "one of the principal rules of religion is to lose no occasion of serving God. And since [God] is invisible to our eyes, we are to serve God in our neighbor: which [God] receives as if done to [God]self in person, standing visibly before us."[2]

So the word from God does not necessarily direct us toward God; by God's own design it directs us toward the world. This being the case, we can also say that while God's word is given to each of us individually, there is an inevitable communal dimension to that word. The word given to us takes into account the multiple words given to our contemporaries; there is an interwovenness in this process, emphasizing the relational nature of existence. Think of it this way: If God gives a word to each moment or each particle of existence, and if this word is always contextualized, then the word always has reference to a community beyond the self. We are never addressed by God as if we were the only creature in the universe: We are addressed by God as a living participant in the fullness of God's creative work. Our response-ability and therefore our responsibility is toward God and the world, and this by God's design. The word is at once individual and communal.

If, then, God's word directs us to the world beyond ourselves, then our faithful response to that word may in fact be our fuller involvement in the world. The concerns we discern in the world might fill our mind and heart, prompting us to responsive action. It is possible that a person can be exceedingly responsive to God's call without even noticing that it is *God's* call. It is, as it were, as if God gives us a gift without a name tag. And this being the case, then once again we can say that God's creative word comes to us as a whisper. So, then, the creative word from God given in every moment is a whispered word, not readily discernible, because it is clothed in the context of our past, because it is a habitual word, because it comes in our preconscious depths, and because it most usually directs us outward to our God-given work in the world. God's word comes to us effectively—it is that which holds us in existence—but it comes to us as a whisper.

In a process world, then, there is no angel without its own whispered word of assurance toward its particular becoming. The word is not often obvious; it is an incarnate word, clothed in the context of the becoming occasion. It is a depth word, inaugurating each moment of existence. It is a habitual word, ever-present, pointing us to a way of being in the world. But it is a word, faithfully given, to every creature in every moment. One can count on it—even in the midst of doubt—for it is not possible to exist without it.

The word is encompassing, empowering, and gracious. It is a word flowing from God's fullness of knowledge of the past from which this new present can emerge; it is a word flowing from God's fullness of possibilities for the future that we may yet become. Thus the word in a sense surrounds us, cradles us, encompasses us through our past and our possible future. Flowing from this encompassing, the word is also empowering. *Because* the word takes in all our circumstances, the word offers us that which we can really become; it is an achievable word, and to that extent it is an empowering word. It directs us in a way in which we can really go! There are no "pie in the sky" illusions in the guiding word of God. Entailed within this empowerment is the graciousness of the word. Because God offers that word, there is a surety to its possibility, and hence the giving of that word is gracious. It follows, then, that trust in God heightens our ability to discern and follow that gracious word. By the grace of God, to be a hearer of the word means that we can also be doers of the word, and not hearers only.

2

The Proclaimed Word

So, then, process theology is very centrally a theology of the Word. But thus far it is a primordial word, universally given, directed to our depths. I hope that by now a particular question has risen in your mind. I have described God's word of creation, by which God continuously calls a world into being. This word is literally the source of our being, without which we would not be at all. But I have insisted that this creative word of God comes to us as a whisper, not always clearly discerned. Its very nature is a kind of hiddenness, so that what we see in daily life is not the creative word of God, but what creation has done with that word in its free responsiveness. And so consider this: If the hidden word of God is supplemented with a revealed word of God and a proclaimed word of God, will not our ability to raise the hidden word of God to consciousness increase? The revealed word and the spoken word together have the power to intensify the whispered word, magnifying its creative power.

The Christian message, of course, proclaims that there is indeed a most precious revealed Word of God, come to us in time, incarnate now not in all the cloaked complexity of multiple pasts, but incarnate in a babe within a manger, grown to a preteen in a temple, and a young man at a baptism. This word revealed in time is of a teacher and preacher and healer who has compassion on the multitudes, nurturing them and us with physical and spiritual bread. This word revealed in time names sin in judgment, forgives sin in mercy, and empowers others to follow him in righteousness. The revealed word culminates in a cross that appears to crush the light and deaden the sound of this word, as if all the sin of the world were sufficient to annihilate the revealed word of God. But this ultimate revelation of God's word is not overcome by death. In the power of God, the word overcomes death itself with new life.

And what is it that this word in time reveals? In Jesus Christ we see the very nature of God revealed, and this nature is of a holiness that judges our sins of exclusion and hatefulness, whether titanic or petty. This nature is of a holiness that reverses our sin-laden values, revealing instead the dignity of God's creation and the will of God toward our communal good. This nature is of a holiness that actually draws us and calls us and empowers us to the creation of a community reflective of God's own image in what Jesus called the *basilea*, the reign of God in our midst. God is revealed to us in Jesus Christ, showing us in shining clarity what we as creatures are called by God's word to be. The good news of the gospel of Jesus Christ is that God's design for creation *can* be fulfilled: We *can* become the redeemed and redemptive people of God. We are invited to share this new life made possible in Jesus Christ; we are invited to participate in God's revealed word, which in turn sensitizes us to that hidden whisper of a word that by God's grace comes to each one of us.

If God's word shows us what we can be, it also shows us simultaneously what and who we are. There is necessarily a judging quality to the word. Let me put it in a rather innocuous way. Supposing that you are a young person, about to graduate from high school. And supposing that you meet an impressive sort of person who is an architect. You have always had an aesthetic appreciation for buildings, finding pleasure in such things as "city walks" just to look at the structure of the various buildings downtown. And you also like to imagine floor plans within the buildings, and wonder what exactly goes into making such things. In conversation with the architect, you mention these interests, and the architect looks at you with a knowing smile and says, "Why not become an architect?"

You hadn't exactly taken your proclivities to such a high-flying notion—an architect! Not only to admire buildings, but to have something to do with their construction! To know what "makes them work" from the inside out! The very idea! But then you crash down to reality—how can you be an architect? You're barely ready to graduate from high school, and without a goal you've not paid much attention to studies. How can you possibly be an architect? And the architect, seeing your despair, keeps smiling. "Well," she says, "there's always summer school, you know, to make up for studies you've neglected—and you can go to community college, and succeed well enough to enter a four-year school where you can major in the necessary field to prepare you for the profession! 'Come on in, the water's fine!'" And her very encouragement is like an empowerment that strengthens your ability to dare the future she embodies.

To be shown a possible future is at the same time to be shown our distance from that future, and also what is needed for its realization. In the same way, to be shown the holiness of the kind of communal life embodied by Jesus is to be shown how far we are from that reality. And yet its very envisagement awakens a longing in us, a yearning not only for its fulfillment, but for our participation in its fulfillment. It may also reveal to us not only how far we are from the vision, but what we have done to prevent its realization. In theological language, to see real holiness is at the same time to see our own sin. The word of the gospel is a judging reality.

But the sake of the judgment is not an end in itself; it is a means to the end of enabling us to become a participant in the reality shown to us in Jesus Christ—a life lived in community, pleasing to God, contributing to the good of this dear earth and all in it. Thus, the revelation of God for us is judging and enabling at the same time; it includes a naming of that which keeps us from the goal, and the enabling forgiveness of sin that wills us toward the goal in spite of our unworthiness. It is a joyful reality, showing us not only what we can be and what we are, but how that gap can be overcome. The word of the gospel calls us to become the people of God, willing and living toward the well-being of creation, living in the grace of community.

But if something like the above is to happen, preaching is absolutely necessary. That is, the enabling revelation of the nature of God that calls us, judges us, and empowers us was given in Jesus Christ 2,000 years ago. Because the revealed word of God in Jesus Christ is a historical word, given in time, preaching is absolutely required as the extension of God's incarnation in Christ across history. Jesus Christ was born in time; his life revealed the nature of God for us, with us. He was crucified, dead, buried, and on the third day rose again. These events happened in a history removed by us through two long millennia.

Most of what happens in history barely survives for two generations as living memory. To be in history for most of us is to be swallowed up in time, all of our significance absorbed in the passage of successive generations. Think of it! How much do you even know of your very own family? What do you know of the passions, hopes, and sorrows of your mother's great-grandmother? Or her great-great-grandmother? Do you even know her name? Or what do you know of your grandfather's childhood? Or his feelings about what mattered to him in his life? Or his father before him? The vital, throbbing matterings of history are finally fragile, lost for the most part in two generations!

If, then, God chooses to be revealed in history, how is this revelation to transcend absorption into the very successiveness of history? The answer, of course, is simple: The revealed word must become incarnate yet again in the proclaimed word. The humble act of preaching, which engages pastors relentlessly week after week, is in fact the "being made present" in history of that word once revealed. Likewise with the sacraments of baptism and the Lord's supper: Each is a representation of Jesus Christ through proclamation, making his reality present to us, making possible our own incorporation into his divine presence. The historical

word made known in Jesus Christ is continuously made
present in history through such humble means.

And why should we be surprised? Do we not celebrate
each year in the festival of Christmas the strangeness that
God-the-most-high chooses incarnation through a baby born
in a stable and placed in a manger? We rightly honor these
things now, so that they hold the aura of holy joy. But a stable?
A manger? God, it seems, is no respecter of proper royal
ways. God chooses ordinary things for extraordinary events.
And so the act of preaching—of struggling with a text, feeling the message, preaching the word—this mundane chore,
this seemingly never-ending event—is today's equivalent of
that stable, that manger. In and through preaching, God's
revealed word in history is revealed yet again in our own
time, time and time again.

And what is its purpose? How does this word once revealed and now proclaimed relate to that whispered word
of God's creation? Remember that God's whispered word
offers ways by which we may deal transformatively with
whatever past we have inherited, whether through our own
doings or the doings of others, and actually, through a com-
bination of both. That whispered word is bound up in the
swaddling clothes of our own particular pasts, limited to
what is really possible for us given the total configuration of
our lives. And to whatever extent possible, that word given
to each of us reflects something of the holy nature of God.
But it is a bound word: bound to our contexts, bound to our
freedom, bound to our own decisions.

The amazing grace of God casts off these swaddling
clothes first in the primal revelation of Jesus Christ, and second, in the preaching of Jesus Christ. Within us the word is a
whisper, dimmed by circumstances and by the clouds of our
own obstructions and repeated rejections—dimmed by sin,
both our own and that of the larger community. In Christ the
word is a shout, showing the holiness of God even in the
midst of history. And in the proclamation of this word
through preaching and sacraments, this word is given in our
own soul's hearing. To hear the word proclaimed offers the

possibility of lifting that hidden whispered word to conscious levels.

Another way to say it requires a brief digression into a cursory discussion of the Trinity. For it may well be that the union of the proclaimed word and the whispered word mirrors in an intriguing way the very dynamic we have long called the trinitarian action of God. We as Christians have long held that God is triune. In the complexities of this doctrine, we have said that while God is indivisibly one, God nonetheless is at the same time three. We have named this threeness "hypostases," or persons, or masks, or centers, or aspects of God, but our language falters because we are trying to name that which is beyond human experience. Our own human mode of being is quite unitarian, for no matter how much "threeness" or "multiplicity" we might find in ourselves (we can be mother or father and preacher and writer at the same time), this does not turn us into a "trinity." But God is so much more than we are that we struggle to express the complexity of how a divine nature might exist. "Trinity" is our way of expressing the "moreness" of God—God is unity and multiplicity at the same time, such that no single individual is sufficient to be an image of God on the human scale—it takes a whole community to be the image of God ("...male *and* female God created them; in the image of God, God created them..." [Gen. 1:27]). Even Jesus, God incarnate for us, does not live the lonely life of an ascetic to reveal God's nature to us, but draws a community around him at the outset of his ministry, and thus lives the community of God even as he preaches the coming of the community as basilea.

So God, as trinity, is in some sense communal at the same time as being deeply, most profoundly one. Our tradition has used the male images of father and son and the female image of spirit to express this muliplicity in God, and further attributed a primacy of creation to one "hypostasis," a primacy of redemption to another "hypostasis," and a primacy of unification (which is also holiness, or sanctification) to yet another "hypostasis." There is a deep fullness to this threefold assignation, for creation is redemptive and unifying, redemption is creative and unifying, and unification is creative and redemptive. Because God is One, the wholeness of God is involved in every act, even though the primacy of the act may be attributed to one hypostasis or another. This trinitarian God who creates a universe, and thus is more than the universe, is also incarnate in the universe. Incarnation occurs in some sense as God offers us guidance in every moment within the depths of ourselves—within the depths of all creation. Through the traditional doctrine of omnipresence, God pervades the universe with divine presence, received by every creature in every moment. But this pervasive presence comes to shining particularity in Jesus of Nazareth. To put it bluntly, it rather boggles our human minds that the creator of the universe who therefore transcends the universe also pervades the universe and is particularly manifest in one Person. We experience God in Jesus Christ as redemptive power, as revelatory power, as saving power. This redemptive power relates to the originating creative power as the grace-laden possibility to correct our refusals of God's creative whispered word, to get us "on track" again in accordance with God's goodwill toward us, for us.

And what of Spirit? Redemption or "correction" is not an end in itself, but a means to the end of community. To become community rather than just a collection of individuals is to be woven together by a spirit of caring for one another in and through God. It is to be so open to the love of God poured out for us in creation and redemption that we ourselves become vehicles of that love toward the greater communal good of the world around us. This is why the unifying power of God is a power toward love, which is the essence of holiness. There is an intimacy to the spirit that creates community, and a shining holiness that seems to yearn that we participate in that holiness by shining with it in our own lives. God as Spirit is that weaving, shining, holy reality that binds us.

The image of God, in which we are created, is not a static image, like some sculpture made of some famous person. Nor is the image of God reflected in the mere fact that we are rational creatures, or free creatures, or any other aspect of what it is to be a human individual. Rather, the trinitarian image of God is reflected in the caring community. This can take place in the intimacy of marriage, or partnership, or friendship, and also in the affectionate binding together in the larger community, such as the church. It can also happen in society insofar as society is just, which is the mode of caring exercised in social living. Caring community, existing in modes of justice, is an image of the trinitarian God, whether that community is large or small.

And what, you might be saying, does this discourse into the Trinity have to do with preaching, thank you? Everything! For in this process theology of the word, I am suggesting that the grand and macroscopic trinitarian work of creating, redeeming, and unifying/sanctifying that we see in the whole wide scope of the universe and history has a microscopic counterpart in us. The same God who calls all creation into being through a word also calls us into being through a whispered word given as the basis of our existence and in the hidden depths of our existence. God the creator is active in us.

The redemptive word of God is given not in the generality of cosmic history, but in the specificity of human history, our history, in the very midst of our existence. But he is other to us, separated in personhood and separated in time; he is Other. We have no access to him unless he is proclaimed, made present to us, which is done in the work of preaching. Through preaching, God as Redeemer is made visible and audible to us, and the distance of history is overcome.

The unifying/sanctifying work of God is the joining within us of the redemptive word preached through the gospel and the creative word whereby God is calling us into being. The work of the Spirit is that inward act whereby the two words become one, reinforcing one another, and empowering us to a fuller responsiveness to God in our lives. The creative word of God whispered in the depths of every individual is paired with the proclaimed word of God, which holds the image of Christ anew before the gathered people. The completion of the preaching act occurs with our openness to the work of the Spirit as the Spirit weaves the spoken and the whispered words together, leading us into grace-full living. Thus, the trinitarian image of God is reflected in the work of preaching.

Something of the very unity of God is shared with us, weaving us into a community called to be holy, called to experience and express the same community-creating love revealed to us in Jesus Christ. As we become community together through the power of the Spirit, we mirror in our finite way the holy community that is the one God, trinitarian, communal from everlasting and to everlasting.

The work of preaching, then, is the proclamation of God's word in history. It is the re-presentation of Jesus the Christ; it is the revelation of who God is for us. As proclamation, it is a participation in the work of the triune God. It is the whisper become a shout, the hidden become revealed, the word made manifest. Preaching is the extension of Christ's incarnation into time, our time.

I have told the story of Augustine and those angels, only some of whom heard the redemptive word. A process theology of the word adapts the story by saying that all creatures exist in and through the word of God and their own responsiveness to it. There is a graciousness to this word of creation, for to be called into existence is itself an amazing grace. But the graciousness of God is such that it goes beyond even this universality. Not content with giving us a word in our depths, even though this word is itself empowering, God gives us a word as well that is received directly into our conscious selves. God works with our depths and with our surfaces, so to speak, toward the end that we might be reflections of God in communities of holiness. And this latter word given to our conscious selves is given in a twofold way. Most wondrously of all, the word is given in Jesus Christ, born humbly in time, raised gloriously to all times. And still wondrously, this word is given through the awesome humbleness and ordinariness of preaching. In the providence of God this word of preaching can become by the power of the Spirit the glorious raising of the community of God in history.

3

The Received Word

Preaching takes place within the context of a theology of the word of God. Preaching is the extension of God's incarnation in the world; it is the re-presentation of the Word made flesh; it is the revealing of the revealed word of God. As such, God uses it to heighten our sensitivity to the hidden word that God whispers to us, calling us into existence moment by moment. The two words meet—the hidden word and the revealed word—by the power of the Spirit in the act of preaching.

Receiving the word, often called being a "hearer" of the word, implies much more than the physical act of receiving sounds through one's ears and interpreting them. A preached word is far more than a series of sounds; it is a total act of communication given in a multiplicity of ways. Speech, whether oral or signed, is certainly involved, but so are the nuances conveyed through the language of one's body. One of the reasons for the great power in signed preaching is the sense in which the whole body is intentionally involved in the preaching event—one preaches with one's whole being, and in so doing, the word is heard in ways deeper than sound. But the full setting of the preaching moment is also part of the communication. The liturgy in which the sermon is embedded and the visible signs and symbols of the holy are all drawn into the event. Preaching is an open act of communication, complex and full. And to grasp this event is to be open to its meaning for one's own life. Receiving the word means comprehending the word; it means awakening to the meaning of the message being conveyed, and integrating this meaning into one's very personhood.

There are at least three issues to be kept in mind to understand the fullness constituting the act of preaching. These are, first, the multiplicity of the sermon; second, the communal nature of the sermon; and third, the way in which this multiplicity and unity work together toward the creation of community.

The peculiarity of sermons is that no two persons in the congregation will hear the same sermon. One sermon is preached; many sermons are heard. In a sense, we all know this. We preach a sermon, whose point seems quite clear to us. And to our surprise (at first), a person in the congregation thanks us for the sermon, speaking with particular gratitude about something we didn't think we said at all! Whose sermon exactly did she listen to? But we graciously express our appreciation, even as we race back in our heads over the actual sermon to figure out where such a message could have been heard.

The process dynamics clarify the multiplicity of the sermon. Preaching is a relational event that involves God, a text, a place, a preacher, a sermon, a congregation, and the persons within that congregation. The sermon as preached is but one piece of the total relational event. To change even one element in this total event is to change the whole. The peculiarity is that perhaps within this confluence of events— God, text, place, preacher, sermon, members of a congregation—the sermon may be the only constant thing! But it is placed within a dynamic configuration relative to each receiver of the word.

Each person comes to the word with a unique past and with quite distinct personal challenges. Remember that each person receives, moment by moment, a whisper from God that calls the person to transformative ways of dealing with his or her past. Every moment presents us with the complex task of responding anew to the shifting winds of our inheritance from the past. Yesterday's problems and joys are somewhat different today.

For example, think of the difference that a week away makes to your renewed approach to your daily tasks. I remember a recent Christmas, when I was looking forward to a week in Kansas with my daughters and their families. All through December I delighted in the anticipation of Christmas week. The anticipation was joyously rewarded—what a week that was! What keen enjoyment pervaded the time, as each day moved toward and then from the celebration of the incarnation of God among us. And now that week is in my past. Remembering it rekindles the warm embers that always glow from the presence of familial love.

Meanwhile, my work went on: I was still the dean of a seminary, organizing the academic life of the school; still a professor with a dissertation or two to read. But my work was not the same as it would have been without that Christmas joy in the midst of my family. The warmth of the occasion isn't separated from my life of work—to the contrary! My very integration as a person means that my family life affects the way I approach and accomplish my professional life, and my professional life informs my family life as well. So when I return to work following the Christmas break, I return with renewed vigor, approaching my work still in the warmth of that wonderful week. My personal circumstances change the context within which I do my professional work.

I recall a quite contrary example. Years ago, when I had just arrived in Washington, D.C., as the dean of Wesley Seminary, the president called for an all-day retreat with his new administrative team so that we could begin to know one another. As it happened, I'd just been informed that morning that my oldest daughter, in the eighth month of her first pregnancy, had been taken to the hospital with a severe case of toxemia. All my alarm signals were going off. And so when the president genially turned to me and said, "Tell us about yourself," I felt paralyzed with horror. The present reality of fear for my daughter was like a clanging symbol, marshaling the emotional baggage from every negative experience of my life. Tell them about myself?! "Which self?" I weakly asked. My personal circumstances changed the context of the question. "Tell us about yourself" immediately upon my return from such a week as Christmas would have been quite a different question from "Tell us about yourself" when my daughter's and grandson's lives were in danger.

Human personality is a deeply complex thing, with a constancy of character that nonetheless responds variously— precisely in and through that constancy—to the continuously changing circumstances of life. We are continuously integrating our immediate and distant pasts in light of fresh possibilities for our present becoming. And this process is guided deeply by the faithfulness of God, who leads us toward our best becoming through that whispered word. God gives us our best "how" of becoming, depending on the shifting variables with which we must deal.

And is this not the zest of life itself? Our lives are not entirely predictable—and they are fragile, in a tough kind of way. We live our lives in confidence and curiosity: confidence, because God is present to us; curious, because we really don't know what's ahead. What we do know is that God knows us and our circumstances thoroughly and, therefore, will guide us faithfully toward the wider good no matter what difficulties we might encounter.

But now consider that this complexity is represented by each person in your congregation. Each comes to the service from a week not necessarily known to you; each brings a newness from that week's experiences; each brings slightly different nuances to old challenges, and slightly different responses to slightly different opportunities. I say "slightly" because usually we work incrementally through the stuff of our lives. We do not often do things by leaps and bounds— and when we do, there has usually been a long, quiet process leading up to the ability to make that leap or that bound. The process of living is a moment-by-moment creative responsiveness to the givenness of our lives, wherein we integrate again and again the stuff from our past, always with an anticipation of what may yet happen. To live is to change. And every person in your congregation is slightly different from the same persons who were in your congregation a week ago. The reality is that no matter how well you know your parishioners, each one is a mystery to you beyond your ken.

When your parishioners gather on a Sunday morning, they each bring their unique immediate and distant pasts. And God, who faithfully works with us, whispers a unique word to each one. They have come to the service for as many reasons as there are persons, but the ostensible purpose is to worship God. To worship God is to open oneself up to God. This can involve gratitude, anger, sorrow, joy—the whole gamut of what it is to feel human emotion. In worship, we intentionally bring who we are to God. Part of the work of worship is that this intended openness to God intensifies the strength of that whispered word. How like this God we worship—we participate in worship to give praise and thanks to God, and in the process, we receive from God the gift of a greater intensity to that whispered word so faithfully given to guide us. In giving to God, we ourselves are gifted.

And in this context you preach a sermon. You have first heard the sermon yourself; you preach it with all the faithfulness you can muster. You proclaim the revealed word of God, and in doing so you are faithful to the nature of God as revealed in Jesus Christ. You may be preaching the prophetic word derived from the gospel that raises all our social norms to question, holding them against Jesus' principles of the reversal of values incumbent upon the reign of God. You may be preaching the power of God, seeking out the lost. You may be preaching the wonder of God's love—but whatever the actual content of the sermon, it will contain within it a witness to the nature of God.

And God, who works with all the influences we receive, guiding us toward integration of those influences for our own communal good, works with your sermon even as God continually fashions those diverse whispered words for each member of your congregation. How God works with your sermon with faithful old Mrs. Brown may be quite different from how God works with your sermon with the new young man in town who just happened to drop in to today's service. They will each hear different sermons, because (1) they hear your sermon in the context of their total situations;

(2) God uses the word you proclaim to intensify the hidden word; and (3) Mrs. Brown and the young man both have the responsibility of integrating what God is doing with the proclaimed and hidden words within their own lives.

This last point is important. You would grossly misunderstand the dynamics of this process if you thought of any individual simply as an automaton, responding by rote to whatever was proposed by God. The dynamism of creation is the freedom that God has built into the heart of creation. We who respond to our various influences, even those from God, are responsible for how we respond. God's guidance for us is given at the initial stages of each of our moments, calling us into being through our responsiveness to that word. But our responsiveness rests with our own freedom. We *must* respond to God's word, but *how* we respond rests within our power. We may conform to the word, or more or less adapt the word to our own purposes, or totally reject the word, even as we depend upon it for our existence. This free responsiveness is one of the variables that enters into the listening process as you preach the sermon.

So, then, the hearing (which is to say, the receiving) of any sermon is a complex, multiple thing. How the sermon is heard depends upon the variable circumstances of the receiver, upon the work of God with that sermon, and upon the freedom of the receiver. The sermon is a relational event, taking place within multiple contexts. Therefore, the sermon, even though it is presented in its own integrity as a single whole, is in reality a multiple event. One preaches as many sermons as there are persons in the congregation. As the common past of the text is held forth, together with the preacher's own responsiveness to that text, God uses both text and sermon to present each person's past in a different light. To put it another way, each one receives the word through the filter of his or her own experience, and through the filter of that whispered word being given by God. Thus, the word that actually reaches each person in your congregation has a highly personal aspect unique to each person. This dynamic lies behind the long-accepted reality among preachers that the sermon a parishioner thanks one for—or criticizes one for!—is not always the sermon one thinks one has preached.

And yet this dynamic presents us with a problem. What saves the sermon from being idiosyncratically split up into as many versions as there are parishioners? What about the congregation as a whole? For if the sermon is a re-presentation of Jesus Christ, and thus an extension of the incarnation into history, it is also the case that the congregation itself, baptized into Christ, is the body of Christ. The congregation is more than a collection of individuals; the congregation is an organic body commissioned to do the work of Jesus Christ in the world. In the multiplicity of the sermon, do we lose the dimension of the unity of the church that allows us to offer the congregation as a whole a direction toward its missional purpose? How is it that the sermon addresses the health of the congregation as a whole, as well as the individual needs of the parishioners?

The dynamics of process thought can be used to bring some illumination to the case. I have emphasized the process dynamics as they apply to individuality, but it's also the case that in process thought individuality is set within a social context. The difference is that the social context is an organic system of relationships and interrelationships in ever-expanding circles. For instance, think about your own situation. You are an individual, but you are a participant in a family with reciprocal relationships. You help shape what the family is, and the family helps to shape who you are. Your family is itself part of still larger networks. The family exists within a loose organization of friendships, both near and distant; and within the context of "place": local, national, and global. Meanwhile, you are also a participant in a professional vocation that reflects the same kind of re-ciprocal dynamics described in relation to the family. If you are a pastor, you are a pastor in relation to a wider church body, be it district, conference, presbytery, synod, or region, which is itself in relation to still larger ways of organizing a national and international church. You are also in relation-ships with other pastors from other denominations who are serving in your town or city. In the denominational and ecumenical contexts, reciprocity exists in various degrees. You represent your own particular denomination and its ethos within your ecumenical relationships. But your experiences in the ecumenical context affect your interactions within your own denomination, perhaps by increasing your appreciation for your familiar ways of doing things, perhaps by giving you a deeper sense of the wider religious context of the body of Christ as a whole. Beyond this, there are the relationships that are developing between you, your church, and leaders and congregations from non-Christian religions within your community. These also affect how you are within your own denominational context, raising new questions or deepening your understanding of your own distinctiveness.

Meanwhile, it is probable that you participate in still other relationships. Perhaps you exercise, working out in a local spa. Or perhaps you participate in some group of political, athletic, or social significance. In all of these cases, your participation in these various forms of organization introduces reciprocity. The influences of each organization affect you in your own self-constitution, and you yourself, whether you notice it or not, have an effect on each organization in which you choose to participate.

What I am describing is an interrelated network of multiple relationships indicating that your existence is far more than individual. You are a communal being, participating in many communities at any moment in your life, and across the length of your life as you grow, move, or simply cut down on one activity in order to make room for another. To be an individual is to be communal.

And your preaching needs to take account of the communal dimensions of living. While your sermon is a multiple thing, heard differently by each member of your congregation, you must remember nonetheless that the congregation as a whole is a community created in and through these members, and in and through multiple relationships that extend beyond the local group. Just as you exist in multiple communal relationships of various importance, so do your participants, and so does the community.

The immediate congregation to whom you preach is a participant within its larger denominational (or, in some cases, nondenominational) body. It is also a participant in a local community, with its own history. Just as the individual participates in multiple organizations beyond the self, even so the communities comprised by individuals gathered together around a common identity and mission participate in organizations beyond themselves. These reciprocal relations define the uniqueness of any body and constitute part of the livingness of that body.

So it happens that while your congregation consists of many individuals, each of whom hears your sermon according to circumstances not wholly known to you, your congregation is at the same time an organic unity, a community. Each member of the congregation has a reciprocal relation with all the others, whether that relation is strong or weak. These relations enter into who each person is, and into the character of the congregation as a whole. The congregation changes with each new member and with the loss of each old member. True, the changes are incremental—we may not immediately notice the effects of these changes. But because of the reciprocity held within the relational identity of the congregation, it shifts and changes according to each addition or deletion. Your congregation is a living organism.

The issue to be raised, of course, is the particular identity of this group. Given the multiple relations in which we engage, why is this congregation a congregation instead of a crowd? What is it that ties this group of multiply related individuals together into this new organic whole called church? What is the binding force? In the midst of all this multiplicity, whence unity, whence community?

Your members have been baptized into Jesus Christ. They are members of the local congregation precisely because they have opened their lives, whether maximally or minimally, to participation in God's incarnate reality. God is revealed in Christ, and in Christ has acted definitively on our behalf. How this action is interpreted has varied through the ages: Often it is seen as "the Great Exchange"—we are identified with Christ so that our sin may be taken by him, and his righteousness may be posited to us. Sometimes this has been portrayed in juridical language: Christ takes the punishment we deserve for our sins. Sometimes it has been portrayed in language of empowerment: To be baptized into Christ is to be empowered by Christ for righteousness. Sometimes it has been portrayed in revelational language: The clarity of God's revelation in Jesus Christ enters into who we are, extending Christ's benefits into our living. But however it has been interpreted, the church has always proclaimed that God in Jesus Christ creates for us a new communal identity. This has been variously named as the image of God, or a reflection of the reign of God, or as becoming the people of God. But however it is named, the reality is that by virtue of our baptism we become not simply a new person, but a new people. We are participants in the continuing incarnation of God as the body of Christ in the world.

But baptism is not a once-long-ago event. It is, by the grace of God, an ongoing event. One is baptized into Christ. But Christ doesn't "stop"; Christ isn't limited to a particular time. Christ is the ongoing revelation of God for us. To be baptized into Christ, then, is an inauguration of a continuing event. We don't say, "I was baptized"; we say, "I am baptized." Through our baptism we are made participants in the resurrected Christ, and are thus constituted as a community.

To be made a participant in Christ has—as one might expect—multiple effects, but one very practical effect is that this participation in Christ fundamentally organizes our personal and communal living. Each of us lives with a particular grid through which we interpret events in our life. Through our baptism into Christ, we are incorporated, even in our diversity, into a shared identity. This identity involves an interpretive grid that organizes our life into meaning in distinctively Christian ways, and directs our life into particular forms of action. Through our baptism we are drawn into a particular way of being in the world. We are made community.

This is not accomplished by some sort of magic. Baptism is not a magical event; it is a communal event. Remember the importance of the congregation's response in the baptismal liturgy? The faith of the congregation is pledged to the support of the one who is baptized, and this pledge is itself part of the baptismal event. This pledge commits the congregation to the task of transmitting to this brother or sister the signs and symbols that orient one's life in Christ toward Christlikeness. This is highly important if the community is to *be* community. Community occurs not by fiat, not by magic, but by participation. The one who is baptized is traditioned into community by the community, and in the process, the community continuously becomes itself. It is community in and through its continuous response to its shared identity in Christ, and one of these responses is its transmission of the stuff of this identity to those who are baptized. Community is a dynamic rather than a static reality and, therefore, must continuously be recreated if its existence is to be sustained.

And here is the role of preaching to the community. That which makes the congregation a community rather than a crowd is a shared identity in Christ, mediated through baptism and through symbol systems that convey not just the intellectual understanding of what God has done for us in Christ, but the emotional nuances and implications of this. And a major factor in mediating this life-orienting comprehension is the sermon.

The sermon, heard by individuals in a multiplicity of ways, is preached to the congregation as a whole. The sermon re-presents Christ, proclaiming to the congregation its shared identity of participation in Christ. Just how this can be done is almost infinite—sermon upon sermon upon sermon can be preached, and still we have not exhausted the content of preaching. But every sermon is marked to some extent as a sermon by the reflection, to whatever degree, of what it means to orient one's life in and around that cluster of meanings conveyed in Christ. Every sermon is identity-forming, re-presenting to the congregation who it is called to be as the body of Christ in the world.

Thus far it may appear that I am arguing two contrary things. On the one hand, I have argued that the sermon is inherently multiple. It is part of many, many relational events. In a relational event, if one portion of that relational event changes, the whole is affected. The fact that each person in the congregation comes to the sermon with a different context that itself varies from week to week means that each person is a variable in the preaching relation. Thus, the congregation can be viewed as a kind of thick overlapping of many relational realities, each of which constitutes a slightly different relational event relative to the sermon. It is thus not possible for two people to hear the sermon in exactly the same way.

But I have also argued that one preaches not to individuals—even though it is individuals who constitute those relational events—but to the congregation as a whole. One preaches to the community, conveying through the sermon in multiple ways what it means to have one's identity in and through the grace of God in Jesus Christ. As such, the sermon is an identity-forming event; it plays an enormous function in the creation of the congregation as community rather than as a crowd of dissimilar people who happen to be together at the same time. How do these two realities come together? What is the connecting link between individuals as hearers-of-the-word and a congregation as hearer-of-the-word? If we all hear a different sermon in multiple ways, how can the sermon at the same time be part of that which creates us as community?

To suggest an answer I remind you again of the work of God. Earlier I used trinitarian language to speak of the creative word of God that comes to each of us as a whisper, and the redemptive word of God that comes to us revealed in the gospel. Traditionally the Spirit has been our way of naming that unitive work of God, springing from the depths of God's nature, that brings about our union with God and our communion with one another.

Imagine it in a fanciful way. Imagine that all those multiple sermons heard as you preach your single sermon are taken by this unitive Spirit by way of application to the internal life of your hearer. The Spirit is selective. For

Mrs. Brown, this particular illustration that you used might speak to her own situation. Perhaps the entirety of the rest of your sermon has simply passed her by, as she sits in the pew and moves from your words in free association to this or that. But you share an illustration—one you almost didn't even include—and it cuts through her random thoughts, bringing her sharply into focus. She does not dwell on your words: rather, she absorbs the force of your illustration, for it suddenly appears to illumine for her the troubles she has been experiencing recently. She sees those troubles in a different light, and somehow they might be a little more manageable. All this time, God has been giving her that whispered word of ways she might work transformatively in and through these troubles. But the word is whispered, opaque. In some way you have re-presented the Christ in that illustration you threw in at the last minute. And the Spirit uses that redemptive word to illumine the whispered word. Mrs. Brown understands. And the Christly identity mediated by your words renews her strength, by the gracious work of the triune God.

Meanwhile, that young man who wandered by also listens to your sermon. He pays little attention to your illustration—he's more interested in what you make of the text. He is a seeker, and in and through your use of that text you are showing him a new way of configuring his identity. He may not apprehend it as such—he is focusing primarily on what it is you are saying about that text. But what is happening to him as he listens to that portion of your sermon is an introduction to a new way of being. His whole world can be reconfigured around this word. What is happening? Implicitly or explicitly, there is a Christly identity being offered to him in the preaching of the word. He may ruminate a bit over the next few weeks concerning the vague responsiveness he experiences within himself in and through that sermon—even if he totally forgets what the sermon was specifically about. What is happening? Because of his presence as you preached, God is able to weave his experience of hearing into a new kind of word to be whispered to him. The proclaimed word makes possible a different kind of whispered word.

But is there a relationship between Mrs. Brown and the young man? Because they are together in this place, there is an effectiveness of each upon the other. It is, after all, a relational world of infinitely complex interweavings of relation and influence, most subliminal. But the common denominator between Mrs. Brown and the young man is the reception of Christly possibilities, each according to her and his needs. The Spirit can lift this common factor, creating a particular relational bond between them of openness. Each is part of the total environment within which the other heard the word; each is therefore part of what God has worked with in eliciting the peculiar responsiveness each has experienced to the word.

I have chosen an illustration of the nameless young man who wandered into the service—but what of Bill and Janet, that stalwart couple within the congregation? What of the relation between Mrs. Brown and Bill and Janet? How do their different hearings make them community? Again, the common denominator is that in and through the representation of Christ in the sermon, they each hear that which makes for Christian identity in their own living. But even though it is variously received, it is a shared symbol system, a shared way of organizing and interpreting experience, a shared way of approaching life's challenges. The Spirit who works with Mrs. Brown is the same Spirit who works with Bill and Janet. If there is a unitive work within each individual, whereby the revealed word is joined with the whispered word to give direction or illumination or reinforcement of a Christly way of life, there is also a unitive work among the individuals who are joined in Christ. In a relational world, they *must* relate to each other, whether at subliminal or conscious levels. The issue is *how* they will relate to each other. Those things that are common to them qualify the relation. Because of their common baptism into Christ, and their common utilization of Christly ways as part of their identity, they are together in Christ. The same Spirit who works unity between the revealed and the whispered word within each person also works unity among those who together participate in that revealed word, Jesus Christ. Through their shared identity, they become community.

But this implies yet one further stage in the preaching process. As the preacher re-presents Christ to the community, knowing that the preaching is part of what the Spirit uses to weld the disparate persons into community, the preacher also must have in view the Christly work of the congregation as a whole within its own interwoven web of relationships with communities beyond its own walls. For just as an individual is a complex and organic unity, existing within multiple situations, the community is a complex and organic unity, existing internally through the reciprocity of relationships among its members, and externally through its reciprocal relations with still other communal organizations. The community, as the body of Christ, is called to extend the work of Christ in the world. The community is called to itself become a sermon in the world, a revealed word in the midst of many whispered words, bringing about transformations toward other forms of community. The congregation as community is an organic body, with a work of God to do in the world. Therefore, one of the responsibilities in preaching is the re-presentation of Christ and his work as the call to the congregation to continue that work within the parameters of its own experienced call to mission.

Being a receiver of the preached word is a multiple and highly complex process. One hears the word relative to one's own personal frame of reference, with a sensitivity to that whispered word faithfully given by God. One hears the word relative to others in the congregation, for in and through the word, one's shared identity with these others is lifted to prominence. And one hears the word relative to the work the congregation is called to do as the extension of Christ's body in the world. A single sermon is preached. Many sermons are heard. In and through the hearing, community is again and again recreated in multiple ways, and new possibilities are opened by God through which this renewed community might be the word of God not only within itself, but also to its many relational worlds beyond its borders.

4

Preaching Theologically

I have stressed that the sermon must in some way offer
the symbols of Christian faith to the congregation, and that
through this the congregation receives the means of continuously reconfiguring its identity as a community in Christ.
What I am calling "symbols" are the great themes of Christian faith: the universe as the creation of God; the problem of
sin; the provision of sin's answer in Jesus Christ who reveals
God to us; the possibility of new life that triumphs over sin;
the creation of community; the work of God through that
community in the world; and the hope of everlasting redemption. A still simpler way of configuring these symbols is
through the imagery of the triune God, insofar as each of the
themes has a primary relationship to God as creator, redeemer, or unifier/sanctifier. I call these themes symbols
rather than doctrines because each can be configured into a
variety of complementing or conflicting doctrines. The symbols are deeper than doctrine or theology, and become the
stuff, the resources, with which theology works. But each
and every theology does something with these symbols, and
thereby constitutes itself as a variation of Christian faith,
Christian identity, and Christian community. The symbols
themselves emerge from the earliest Christian communities
and are encoded in the Christian canon, our scriptures.

The story of the tradition is the weaving of these symbols into now one configuration and now another in a variety
of trajectories. Christian identity is largely a function of how
the symbols have been woven theologically within a

particular trajectory within the wider tradition, and even more so, within the countless lives and congregations making up that trajectory. Christian living is informed by the symbols of Christian faith, in whatever theological form their organization may take. It's as if we are describing a family tree, with the fundamental symbols of Christian faith forming the trunk, and the various theological interpretations of these symbols, the branches. We can imagine three great branches as Catholic, Protestant, and Orthodox, but each of these branches yields yet other variations. Within Catholicism, there are various orders; within Protestantism, there are various denominations; within Orthodoxy, there are various nationalities. And so each branch branches off yet again, manifesting the tree's growth and vitality. But each branch, whether large or small, owes its existence not to itself, but to the trunk that supports the branches—and to the deep roots of God's work with us that allows the growth of the tree in the first place.

If the branches are the theological interpretations of the symbols, one might ask, Why not simply stay with the symbols? Isn't that simpler, easier, and closer to the root experience of God's work? But the paradox is that the symbols cannot simply be given as they are, in their rawness. To give them is to interpret them. This is theology. And since the symbols emerge from the texts as interpreted by the traditions, both text and tradition are important to theological preaching.

The rich story of text and tradition is not a closed story, with "The End" written neatly at the end of it. As a grandmother I have often told stories to rapt grandchildren, who listen to me wide-eyed, never taking their gazes from my face until finally I have woven the tale toward its conclusion, pronouncing it so with a very solemnly uttered, "The End." There is no doubt in my children's minds that the story is indeed over. But there is no "The End" to the story of how text and tradition merge in the continuous creation of Christian community. To the contrary! Every new generation has the responsibility of paying attention to its past in order to adapt the symbols to a new chapter in the never-ending story. Its own adaptations are its own formation of communities of witness and service, and its gift to the generations that will succeed it.

To be a student of theology is to learn that Christianity is a tradition that is constantly in the process of transforming itself. Nearly every major theologian whom we now revere was, in his or her own time (the remarkable fact that the writings of a number of women mystics have been preserved allows me to use both pronouns), embroiled in controversy over his or her particular way of putting things. Those theologians most responsible for what have become today's various Protestant denominations did so through their singular reinterpretation of the tradition each had received: Luther's emphasis on salvation through faith alone; Calvin's understanding of predestination; Wesley's interpretation of sanctification; Campbell's emphasis on the ministry of all believers—these and others were not simply repetitions of what had been said earlier. Each was an innovation strong enough to inaugurate a new community of distinctive Christian witness. Each received scornful invectives and charges of being "unchristian" and "heretical," yet each contributed to significant transformations within the ever-in-process Christian tradition.

The Christian tradition is a living thing. By definition, to be living is to be dynamic, which is to be continuously in the process of receiving from the past, critically integrating that past in light of the contemporary situation, and giving one's newness to the future. Each generation of Christians receives from the past, integrates it into present experience with some degree of novelty, and shapes the kinds of transformations that might happen in the future. In most cases, the changes are incremental, not immediately apparent. But part of the wonder of those geniuses who arise within the tradition is that they are able to receive and critically integrate the tradition in fresh ways that adapt that tradition more adequately to their own time. The living nature of Christianity wrestles with the new interpretation, quarrels with it, struggles against it, and is finally illumined by it as once again it undergoes a radical transformation. The transformations are witnesses to its life. Only a dead tradition is impervious to change.

So pastors must offer the symbols of Christian faith as mediated through texts and traditions to congregations, modeling for congregations the challenge and excitement of thinking about those symbols in light of the contemporary context. Remember, it is precisely through these symbols, theologically interpreted, that God forms persons into communities, and forms the communities into agents for mission in the world. Through these symbols we learn who we are and what, as communities, we are called to be and do. Thus, every sermon must deal with some aspect of these symbols, which is to say that every sermon must be theological.

But precisely how do we preach theologically? Do we get out our old theology texts from seminary days, dust them off, and plow back into them? While no seminary professor of theology would wish to discourage such diligence, it may not be so complicated as that! Instead, keep in mind the great symbols as summarized earlier: the universe as the creation of God; the problem of sin; the provision of sin's answer in Jesus Christ who reveals God to us; the possibility of new life that triumphs over sin; the creation of community; the work of God through that community in the world; and the hope of everlasting redemption. There are few biblical texts that do not deal with one or more of these symbols. So my suggestions are: (1) Read the sermonic text, whether from a lectionary or otherwise, to uncover the fundamental symbol encoded in that text. (2) Treat yourself to your own history! Do some background study on how that symbol has been appropriated within your own branch of the Christian tradition! (3) Weave text and tradition together, or contrast the text with the tradition, or let the contrasts and/or conflicts within the text and the tradition push toward yet one more transformation of the symbol involved.

Let me illustrate the above through a familiar gospel text. John 9 tells the story of Jesus' healing of the man born blind. The story begins with Jesus seeing the blind man, and then being questioned concerning the reasons for the blindness: "Who sinned?" ask the disciples. Jesus separates the issue of blindness from sin, announces that the works of God will be displayed in the blind man, and proceeds to give him sight. From there the story shifts from what Jesus does, to what happens to the now-seeing man. His identity is doubted, his word is doubted, and his faith is doubted—he evidently receives a lot of trouble along with his sight! But he steadfastly asserts that he is himself, that he had been blind, and that Jesus, who had made him see, was from God. Nonetheless, he is driven out, and then found again by Jesus. Jesus reveals that he is the Son of man, that he judges the world, and that spiritual seeing is more than a matter of physical sight.

What are the symbols within this text? At least three are from my list: the problem of sin; the provision of sin's answer in Jesus Christ who reveals God to us; and the possibility of new life that triumphs over sin. The text holds the symbols within a narrative form, thus giving them the concrete richness of the story. Supposing, then, you select the issue of sin. The story refutes the causal connection of sin with punitive suffering, which is interesting in itself since so much of the tradition equates sin and suffering. Even so great a theologian as Augustine says "all evil is the result of sin and its punishment." But here the text itself refutes the tradition. Within the text, sin is not associated with the suffering of physical blindness—rather, sin is associated with lack of spiritual understanding, referred to in the text as "spiritual blindness."

And here a problem arises. The text is quite clear: A person who is incapable of seeing physically but who sees quite well spiritually is contrasted with persons who see quite well physically, but who willfully refuse to see spiritually. An innocent physical blindness is contrasted with a sinful spiritual blindness. In the context of John 9, the contrast works powerfully. But throughout our long tradition we have too often taken blindness itself, rather than spiritual blindness as in the text, to be symbolic of sin. This does great disservice to those who are physically blind, forcing them into the role of symbolizing sin! It also does disservice to the text, for the blind man sees spiritually prior to restoration of physical sight; his physical blindness is spiritually pure. When we follow this text, then, we must make it plain that the refusal to see spiritually is the problem; hence it is not against blindness per se that we are cautioned, but against a willful "spiritual blindness."

What, then, is "spiritual blindness"? In this text it appears to have multiple forms. It is bias that prevents granting credibility toward another; it is the willingness to revile and persecute those with whom one does not agree; it is the refusal to recognize one's own participation in sin; and it is the refusal to recognize the works of Jesus as being from God.

To preach from the text theologically, then, could mean to explore the meaning of sin that is put forward within the text. But just as the Pharisees within the text are portrayed as insisting that *their* way of seeing Jesus should be the way the man who was born blind should see Jesus, even so we can immediately pour our own assumptions into each of these forms of "spiritual blindness." "Aha!" we can crow, "of course! The text associates 'spiritual blindness' with refusing to grant credibility to a faithful witness. Mr. Jones refused to believe Mr. Smith; Mr. Jones is therefore 'spiritually blind,' and needs this text!" While this is clearly a caricature, the text nonetheless cautions us not to move too quickly in assuming we know what its symbol can mean.

Is "spiritual blindness" spoken of in other texts? The story of Simon the Magician in Acts 8 comes to mind. Simon professes faith for the sake of the power and prestige it can give him—he fails to see that "signs and wonders" are not for the sake of one's own prestige, but for the sake of creating community. In 2 Corinthians 4, Paul speaks of "spiritual blindness" in connection with failure to see the work of God in Christ. The writer of 1 John 2 associates "spiritual blindness" with the refusal to love one another. By checking out other passages that also deal with the particular issue yielded by the primary text, we are led into deeper nuances of the symbol. Returning to John 9, the question then becomes whether or not the meanings suggested in these other passages can illumine the meaning in John.

But there is a further way to gain insight into the symbol of sin as "spiritual blindness," and that is to see how it has been interpreted within the tradition. For example, the text associates "spiritual blindness" with refusal to grant credibility to another, and within the tradition John Wesley associates spiritual pride with the refusal to learn from another—even from those with whom we disagree theologically![3] This is an instance of the text and the tradition reinforcing one another.

To go beyond just those theologians within the tradition whose work you happen to know, it is wise to check the wider resources. I have often recommended a particular reference text to my students, even though that text was written one hundred years ago. It is Reinhold Seeberg's *Textbook on the History of Doctrine,* published by Baker House. The volume is in two parts: Part 1 gives a history of doctrinal development up to the Reformation, and Part 2 picks up the story, taking it through the nineteenth century. The book is bedside reading only if one has insomnia. The real wonder of the book is its amazingly detailed index. For example, to look up "sin" is to find a reference to the peculiarities of how sin has been interpreted throughout nineteen centuries of Christian history. And it is a fascinating experience to move from the index to the various pages, reading the variations on the theme as our theological forebears wrestled with the issue of how to interpret sin, and the relation of sin to suffering—and to ignorance, which in some cases is spiritual blindness.

In addition to the value of such a text as Seeberg's, there are also the contemporary books. Now is the time to take down that favorite theologian, and to see how he or she understood the nature of sin. The index can be your guide as you familiarize yourself again with a particular theology. And what of specifically homiletical guides, such as Kathy Black's *A Healing Homiletic: Preaching and Disabilities?*[4] Resources abound!

Sometimes text and tradition contrast with one another, such as the difference between this text dissociating sin and suffering, and Augustine who traces all suffering to sin. And sometimes text and tradition reinforce one another, such as Wesley in his own variation of sin as the refusal to grant credibility to another. But what about those instances when both texts and traditions seem counter to contemporary theological sensitivities? What of texts with which we simply disagree? What then?

Take, for instance, the text of Abraham sacrificing Isaac. The story as recounted in Genesis 22 portrays God as putting Abraham to the supreme test of sacrificing Isaac as a burnt offering to God on a distant mountain. What text could be more poignant than Isaac's, "My father! Behold, the fire and the wood, but where is the lamb for the burnt offering?" Subsequently Abraham and Isaac reach the appointed place, and Abraham binds Isaac, laying him on the altar on top of the wood. As his hand is raised to kill the youth, an angel stops him and points to a ram caught in a nearby thicket, and the ram is sacrificed in place of Isaac.

The text is taken by Christians in two primary ways: One way is to demonstrate the obedience proper to faith; another way is to look at the text symbolically as foreshadowing Christ as our substitute offering for sin. But both of these uses of the text create problems.

Søren Kierkegaard points out the difficulties in taking the Abrahamic text as a lesson in obedience. In *Fear and Trembling*, Kierkegaard plays with the story of Genesis 22 by supposing that a parishioner, hearing the story, decides that God has also spoken to him, telling him to take his own son and to kill him as an offering to God. Kierkegaard spins out a number of variations on the theme of the deranged parishioner, asking how we are to respond to irrational dictates of faith. How are we to determine whether a religious intuition is the voice of God or some diabolical misdirection? What is the criterion for determining the voice of God?

If we look to the ministry of Jesus for our criterion, we could say that love for God in and through love for others is our criterion. Jesus always acts toward the well-being of the other, disregarding society's boundaries that say "thus far well-being, and no farther!" Jesus reached across all boundaries, extending well-being. But how do we apply this criterion to the obedience in the Abrahamic text? Abraham, in obedience to God, prepares to kill his son: Is this action toward the well-being of his son? And even if we say, "Ah, but Abraham loved God so much that he was willing to give up that which he loved best in the world!" we are not exactly off the hook, for Abraham's "giving up" of Isaac was to kill him. Is this what love for and obedience to God require?

Perhaps if we look to the second typical theological response to the Abrahamic text we may find our resolution. For much of the Christian tradition has understood the basic symbol within this text to be a prototype of God's provision of sin's answer in Jesus Christ, who reveals God to us. Thus, the text is taken as a foreshadowing of God sending Jesus to a designated mountain—Golgotha—there to be slain as a sacrifice for sin, and as a substitute for us. "Vicarious atonement" is the doctrinal formulation of the symbol, and it achieves one of its most influential expressions in Anselm of Canterbury's small book, *Cur Deus Homo?* or Why did God become human? Using law court imagery, Anselm argues that we have committed an infinite sin against God by refusing God the honor due to divinity. Our sin must be balanced by a payment adequate to the cause. However, in our fallen state, we are incapable of paying such a debt. In fact, only an infinite being could make adequate satisfaction for an infinite sin! But in justice, since it was a finite being who committed the sin, it must be a finite being who pays the recompense. Obviously this is a no-win situation. But just as the angel provided the ram, even so God provides the only possible substitute: God, in the second person of the Trinity, becomes finite in order (1) to render perfect obedience to God, which is to show God due honor, and (2) having incurred no guilt of sin himself, he dies anyway as a sacrifice for sin. But of course since he is God incarnate, he is infinite; therefore, it is an infinite sacrifice rendered by one who is at once infinite and finite.

The "law-court" imagery of God exacting God's just due in Anselm's doctrine deeply influenced the subsequent tradition, even while the language for sin underwent variations. Whether one knows Anselm's works or not, a Christian can hardly read Genesis 22 without seeing it in terms of Jesus Christ provided as a sacrifice for sin. If we go back to the text, however, a rather curious piece of information emerges. The book of Leviticus gives a careful description of burnt offerings for sin, and the animal to be offered is either a bull or a female lamb or goat, not a ram. A ram was to be offered only for unintentional misdeeds, such as might have been appropriate for the boy Isaac in the story. If the Genesis text is indeed to bear the burden of symbolizing Christ as the sacrifice for all the egregious sin of the entire world, wouldn't a bull or female lamb as a sin offering have been more appropriate to the imagery? The imagery of the text jars with the imagery of the tradition.

Sometimes, when a given theological interpretation of a text seems to lead to insurmountable problems, it is wise to see if there are other symbols within the text that might lead us in more fruitful directions. For example, we can also see encoded within the Abraham story the symbol of life triumphing over death—in this case through pronouncing an end to child or human sacrifice. Indeed, since child sacrifice was a common practice within the Abrahamic time period, such a text would have been liberative. Some contemporary theologians such as Delores Williams argue even further that perhaps human sacrifice is abolished for all time—not to be brought in again as legitimating the tortures of crucifixion, but as abolished, period! Perhaps putting people to death to please God is a human rather than divine idea! Rather than legitimating the sacrifice of any human, whether Isaac or Jesus, maybe the text is telling us that God is for life. There is many a companion text for such a theme. For example, the book of Romans declares that although we put Christ to death, God raised him up! And nothing can separate us from the love of God in Christ, not "death, nor life, nor angels, nor principalities, nor things present, nor things to come, nor powers, nor height, nor depth, nor any other created thing shall be able to separate us from the love of God which is in Christ Jesus our Lord" (Rom. 8:38–39).

If we take the symbol of God's triumph over death to be encoded within Genesis 22, then we will associate the text not primarily with crucifixion, but with resurrection. It becomes an Easter text. Its corollary passages are those such as Romans 8. A study of the tradition relative to this theological use of the text will be guided by resurrection as transformation. And with regard to the reading that takes the text to be a lesson in obedience, we can read that obedience—as do many Jewish commentators—as Abraham's learning *not* to sacrifice Isaac. Our stress should not be on his willingness to sacrifice Isaac, but on his ability to turn from this willingness to find an alternate way. Obedience is measured by responsible caring for the well-being of others.

Instead of allowing the complexity of the issues to discourage preaching theologically from the texts, I suggest that this very complexity can make preaching challenging and freeing. Being a New Testament church endorses theological diversity in the church and frees us to think and preach theologically. It's as if the texts themselves invite us into the adventure of thinking theologically, with room for experimenting with ways of expressing God's work for us, daring to follow suggestions, make mistakes, back up, try again, always attempting to go deeper. By including divergent theologies, and thereby laughing—maybe gently, maybe riotously—at our demand for absolute accuracy in our theological way of expressing God's work, the texts invite us to trust God more than the texts; they point us beyond themselves to the reality of a life of faith that trusts God enough to dare to think. The texts present the organizing symbols of Christian faith, and lure us into the joy of interpreting them in our own time for the sake of the work of God in the world.

If the texts contain the seeds—or the actuality—of divergent theologies, it is highly unlikely that a reader will find every text to his or her liking. For example, we are jarred rather than inspired by Paul's conclusion to his otherwise magnificent Romans 12. He has lifted us to heights of wonder as he describes a holy life. In echoes of the Beatitudes he tells us to bless those who curse us, bless, and curse not. Feed your enemy if that person hungers; give water where there is thirst. And why? Here is where the great apostle shocks us: "For in doing so you will heap burning coals upon his head." Happily, he immediately follows this with the injunction to "not be overcome by evil, but overcome evil with good." Yet we wonder: How is it good if we do good to our enemies *because* it hurts them? Rather than trying to justify Paul's sentiment, we often slide over his comment, breathing a sigh of relief when he returns to his holier rhetoric.

Psychologically, it may indeed be quite difficult for our enemies when we show ourselves to be of a more generous spirit. Shall we excuse the apostle for his remark on the grounds that he was simply making an astute observation? But the plainer meaning of the text is that the enemy should receive not only our own wrath (expressed in holy ways, of course) but that the enemy should also receive the wrath of God. There is no hint here that we should examine our own consciences to see if there be any fault in us! Furthermore, if the generosity we show in treating our enemy well is merely a weapon of "one-up-manship," it is hardly generosity at all. So we are left with a text with which we disagree. What do we do?

The most sensible response is honesty. The age of the Bible was no sanctified period when all persons—especially those involved in writing the texts—felt holy thoughts and did pious actions. To the contrary, folks were just as conflict-ridden and subject to the full gamut of human emotion and cultural prejudice as we find in our own age. How odd it would have been had such feelings been written out of the texts, as if somehow in that day, as opposed to our own, the Holy Spirit was so successful with the human community that nothing ever went wrong, and no spiteful thought ever passed one's conscious attention. Why must we baptize vindictiveness just because it is written into the Bible? Or why should we baptize prejudice, or hatefulness, or wrongheadedness, or errors just because they make their way into a text? Perhaps God intends us to use our heads as we read the texts, to think, to ponder, and to make judgments. Perhaps we never were intended to read the texts slavishly, as if no more thinking had to be done on a subject! Here we would do well to learn from Judaism's age-old tradition of viewing texts as starting points, not stopping points, for thinking about a life of faith. Of course the texts provoke us! They goad us into thought.

So when you disagree with the theology in a text, whether that theology be implicit or explicit, pick up the challenge and figure out on what basis you disagree. Where does this text push you in terms of the continually transforming

Christian tradition? Don't ignore the text! Quarrel with it;
struggle with it; probe it for the thinking the text forces you
into. Perhaps your struggle will lead you to acquiescence,
or perhaps your struggle will lead you to some adaptation,
or perhaps your struggle will lead to outright rejection, which
is itself a form of faithful transformation. Let such struggles
be background to your sermon presentation, as part of the
background from which the sermon emerges. And when you
preach the sermon, let the symbols themselves take the fore-
ground, inviting the congregation into its own theological
work.

We have a fairly good precedent for arguing against the
theology in a text in Martin Luther, who was so disgusted
with the book of James that he called it no more than "a book
of straw." James's emphasis on being "doers of the word,
and not hearers only" smacked too much of "works righteousness" to the great Reformer. Was Luther right? In my
own opinion, he was not: There is much solid theology in
the book of James. But I am glad Luther disagreed, for out of
his vehement rejection of James we get his magnificent com-
mentary on books like Galatians! Do not worry when you
secretly find yourself in disagreement with a text. Take it as
God's opportunity and challenge to think more deeply into
how and why you think we must take a different theological
approach today.

As you do so, you will notice that you, like Luther, are
working with some criterion for determining the compara-
tive importance of the various Scriptural texts. For Luther,
that criterion was "Christ and his benefits." By this he meant
salvation by faith alone, offered graciously by God based
upon the efficacious work of Jesus Christ. Luther judged the
importance of every text according to this criterion. He val-
ued each text that illumined or supported this doctrine, and
questioned those that appeared to question its primacy.

We, too, bring theological criteria to our reading of the
text, and we need to make our own criteria explicit. For some,
like Luther, that criterion is distinctively related to a
particular interpretation of justification by faith. This then
becomes the organizing center of all Christian symbolism,

whether textual or theological. For others, such as Walter Rauschenbusch, the criterion is drawn from the ministry and message of Jesus. Jesus' unparalleled example of extending care to marginalized or outcast persons in society is taken as the primary sign of the reign of God.[5] For Rauschenbusch this reign of God became the organizing center of theological symbols and the criterion for interpreting the importance and application of all texts. Still another organizing center might be found in the resurrection of Christ, with its organizing motif of creative transformation. John B. Cobb, Jr., is an example of a contemporary theologian whose organizing motif is creative transformation.[6] No evil is final, for God is the power of transformation even in the most hellish of circumstances.

These various criteria are not necessarily mutually exclusive, nor are they exhaustive. But whatever our criteria may be, if we intend theological faithfulness in our preaching ministries, we must identify our own criteria. How do we organize the symbols of Christian faith and practice? Naming this can help us find our way through the maze of differences and challenges within the texts. It will also help us to work responsibly with the symbols within the texts we preach, even as we pull the symbols into theology according to the criteria we bring, and according to our perception of the needs in the congregation to whom we preach.

So, then, being aware of our own theological sensitivities, we should approach a sermonic text prayerfully. The open inquiry of a prayerful reading of the texts makes room for God's guidance as we read; there is an illumining power that can take us deeply into these words of our ancestors in the faith, who attempted, like us, to give a reason for faith. While reading, watch for the great symbols of the Christian tradition within the text: the nature of God; the human condition; what God has done for us in Christ; God's continuing presence with us through the Spirit; and God's goals for us in this life and in the everlasting life that is our end.

We cannot approach a text as if we were encased in some vacuum tube that strips us of our own time and place. It's more as if the glasses we use when we read the text are supplied for us not only by our own place in history, but also by the particular issues that grip us in our own lives, or the life of our congregation. Sometimes the context is an event on the international or national scene. And when we read the text through glasses provided by our own context, we might find ourselves studying with double vision. On the one hand, we will be reading with a view of the past as given through historical study of the text and its theological themes. But on the other hand, we read with a view colored by the urgency of the present. And there will be a convergence, so that the contemporary issue will give a different perspective on an ancient doctrine, or an ancient doctrine will give illumination for a contemporary issue. Our task is to be faithful to both, to study the text and its own context as faithfully as possible. But this faithfulness also calls upon us to know our own context and to be clear about the weaving we do as we entwine the two contexts.

With regard to the personal rather than social context, while each of us is individual, there is so very much we share that no one journey is isolated. The things that trouble me trouble others as well. There are others in a congregation who face the same struggles as the preacher. The context of all our sermons is not only the text and its immediate and subsequent history; it is not only the issues in contemporary society; it is the issues that engage our own souls. In a sense the sermon is always preached first to the preacher. And having felt the sermon as it preached itself to us, we earn the right to preach it to others.

As a lay theologian, then, I encourage pastors to take us all, and themselves as well, more deeply into the faith that God is for us. Congregations need a theological literacy about who we are as God's peculiar people; we need food for our intellects that goes beyond "baptized common sense"; we need the deep things of God. Insofar as preachers immerse themselves in the text, the historical context, and the contemporary context, they will find themselves growing theologically. And in their own growth, by the grace and love of God, they will discover that their congregations will grow as well.

5

Letting the Sermon Go

A major principle to remember for every sermon we write or preach is that we must let the sermon go, for at least three reasons: metaphysical, practical, and theological.

We put so much effort into writing sermons that it's not surprising we think of them as "our" sermons. In a sense, of course, they are: But they are so much more. Consider the rhythm involved in preparing and delivering a sermon. First, there is the act of receiving the sermon in the very process of its creation. We ourselves are the first "hearers" of the sermons we preach. We immerse ourselves in a text, reading it over and over until it pulsates in our own consciousness. But we read that text within the context of ourselves and our congregations.

With regard to ourselves, our own needs, challenges, and joys are never far from the surface when we go to the text. We, as much as anyone in our congregation, need to hear a timely word. And so, as we immerse ourselves in the text and do the requisite reading about the text, its application to our own situations comes into view.

The peculiarity of any scripture text is its fluidity. It is as if the text always reaches beyond itself into the lives of its hearers. This living nature of the texts is not some transhistorical magic somehow contained within these ancient writings. The living nature of the texts is the time-worn patina that comes from persons in every millennium and century and decade and year and month and week and day and hour and minute and second of the tradition encountering these same texts. In that encounter, the text is read from a context that enters into the reading of the text itself. Between text and context, a timely word emerges that speaks directly to the hearer. The paradox obtains that every age reads a "different" text, even while reading the same words. There is a fluidity to the text built up over endless ownings, endless adaptations, and endless sermons from the text addressed by the mercy and grace of God to the peculiarities of time and place and person.

And so when we go to the text for our sermon, we enter into that stream of tradition, hearing a word that addresses ourselves. We bring our loneliness to the text; our "too-much-to-do-and-not-enough-time-to-do-it-in-especially-not-in-this-sermon" to the text; our joys-in-relationship or our sorrows-in-relationship; our zest for ministry or our discouragement in ministry or simply our complacency with ministry; our anger, our umbrage, our pride, our humility, our complexity, our simplicity—we bring ourselves to the text. And the word weaves itself around our condition, delivering to us its timely word. Thus, we ourselves are the first hearers of the word; we who write the sermons are ourselves its first recipient.

But there is more than that. We bring not only our own lives to the text, but we bring into our reading the lives of those for whom we prepare the sermon. We know our congregations. We see our people in that way peculiarly known to anyone in authority, even when that authority is collegial and empowering. We see the pettinesses and the generosities, the will-to-power and the heart-to-serve, in all the intricate weaving of relation upon relation that constitutes a congregation. We bring the individual members of the congregation and our knowledge of the personality of the congregation as a whole to our reading. This context, as well as the context of our being, enters into our reading, and so we read not simply for the sermon we ourselves need to hear, but for the sermon emerging in relation to the congregation.

And so, given the complex intensity and work that we bring to our reading of the text, why isn't it "our" sermon? If the "our" is intended communally, we are right, but if it is intended individually toward the self, it is wrong. We go to the text, and in and through our wrestling with the text, we receive a sermon addressing us, which itself then weaves into a sermon addressing the congregation. For all our work, the sermon is nonetheless first of all a gift, given by the Spirit in and through our work with the text.

But if it is gift, is it not ours? Yes and no. Yes, the sermon is ours—but it is ours to give away. I remember when I was writing my first book, *God Christ Church*—in Paris, of all places! I met my friend, Barbara, when we were classmates at Pomona College. Our friendship is such that we "spark" each other's minds, and we thought of going to her mother-in-law's beach house in Maine where we could each do our writing in conversation with the other. "Why don't we go to Paris, instead?" said Barbara, who is a historian of French anarchy. Why not indeed! And so we went to Paris, and I began writing my first book. But I got stuck on the chapter on the church. Things had gone swimmingly (more or less) until this chapter needed to write itself. What to do! And so I went to Notre Dame cathedral to think it over.

Sitting there in that glorious witness to a millennium of Christian worship, I absorbed its beauty. The windows, the soft organ music, the wonderful old stone of its walls, all began whispering to me of the church, and as I sat there the chapter on the church began to write itself within me. I remember the almost-comical sensation of slowly rising from my place and walking the few blocks back to the apartment. I needed to keep the words inside my head until I could write them down, and my image was to keep my head absolutely upright lest the words should tumble out my ears and be gone! I had to keep the words until I could give them away! But once they were written, they were no longer exactly my words anymore. They belonged to whoever read the book. They were mine only to give away.

And the same thing is so with our sermons. They are ours to give away. Given, they are no longer ours. Our sermons are given to us in trust for the congregations to whom they belong. Our responsibility is to receive the sermon and to give it away.

By now you can probably intuit the metaphysical reasons for this dictum that we must let the sermon go. Remember the fundamental dynamic of all things. To exist is to receive the influences from the past, along with a whispered word from God as to how those influences might be handled. There is then the process of integration, which is the way each bit of existence responds to God's word *and* its past as it goes about the task of pulling that past together. Then there is the moment of transition, when what has been done is given to the future. The motion, then, is to receive, to integrate, and to give, repeated again and again and again in the multiple processes of existence.

This dynamic applies to the tiniest and simplest of things, such as a quark, and to what we conceive to be the most complex of things, ourselves. If one were to go into the metaphysics of it, there would be all sorts of qualifications, tracing the differences between a single organism such as a quark and complex embodied organisms like ourselves. But these distinctions do not eliminate the basic dynamic of existence: receiving, integrating, giving.

I call to your attention that this dynamic means that all existence is intensely relational. Receiving is relationship, for it takes that which is other to the self into the self. Relationships enter into us formatively, both physically and psychically. The most isolated of recluses is yet relational, existing in and through the manner by which he or she pulls the energy of others into the self. Isolation is no protection from the inexorable reality of relation.

The process of integrating is likewise relational. Integrating relationships is that deep act of internalizing the external influences one receives. Have you ever noticed how you tend to talk to yourself, formulating sentences within your head even when you are alone? An internal dialogue of some sort is quite rational, since we are always in the process of internalizing external relationships. In a sense, those whom you are mentally addressing *are* present, albeit only by way of influence. Their subjectivity is elsewhere—but their effect is internal! And so you quite naturally formulate your feelings into thoughts in internal dialogue. (Of course, internal dialogues are much easier to manage than external dialogues, since we can fill in exactly the response we know we can handle!)

The final phase, giving, is also intensely relational. To whom do you give? The staggering reality, in a relational world, is that you give to the entire universe. This is not just a fanciful statement. We exist in so thoroughly a relational creation that everything affects everything else. I've often repeated my physicist brother's poetic words, "You are stardust." In one of the illustrations in his book, *Conceptual Physics*, he has a photo of his grandson, with a comic-strip balloon drawn into the photo. The words he then puts in little Alec's mouth are: "Atoms are so tiny that I inhale billions of trillions with each breath, nearly a trillion times more atoms than the total population of people since time zero! In each breath, I inhale billions of atoms exhaled by every person whose breaths are now evenly mixed in the air. So there are atoms in my body from every person who ever lived, excepting newborn babies far away. But atoms I've recycled are now part of them. From a physics point of view, we're all one!"[7] As Christians, we should be a bit awed to acknowledge that the very molecules of air breathed by Jesus Christ now form part of who we are—and who everyone else is. To exist is to be physically related to the whole universe; to exist is to receive from all and to give to all. Everything that will come into existence will to some degree or other be affected by you: who you are, what you do. Oh, to be sure, the effect may not at all be what we like to think about as fame, or even notoriety! Luckily, we hardly notice most of these effects because they are simply the physical reality of interrelational existence. But the fact is, you actually make a difference in the world, and by making that difference, everything else must take your existence into account and integrate some facet of your influence into its own becoming.

This reality at the level of physical existence is replicated in the area of meaning. Who you are in your own and in others' interpretation of you makes a difference in this world. *That* you will have an effect on everything and everyone else rests with the sheer physics of existence; *what* that effect will be rests upon the type of influence you create in and through your own intentions. What you make yourself to be, you give influentially to others, whether for good or for ill.

And so, when we move from this fundamental relational dynamic of the universe to the simple (or not-so-simple) act of preaching, we underscore the reality that you will give your sermon away whether you want to or not, so you might as well do so intentionally! Preaching enters into the dynamic of existence; it is an integration of influences from text and context that, having become integrated into just this sermonic form, must now be given away. You give it away formally when you preach, but of course at a more fundamental level you give it away even as you experience it yourself within your own hearing, your own being. Metaphysically speaking: Let your sermon go.

The practical reason for giving your sermon away has already been dealt with to some extent in the earlier chapter on being receivers of the word. But there is more to be added. In preparation for these thoughts on preaching, I asked several people what in fact they look for in a sermon. Sharing some of that information with you may illumine some of what it means to give your sermons away.

"What makes a sermon meaningful to you?" I asked. Granted, my survey pool was random and totally too small to qualify for Gallup. "I want to hear something about the texts" was echoed a number of times. The texts have a critical place within our tradition. And while indeed the compilation of the texts was a relatively late selection from a great diversity of texts in the early church, so that the texts themselves are created in and through the tradition, we people of the Reformation give a peculiar primacy to the word contained in the Old and New Testaments. The laity who named this desire to hear sermons based on the text (as opposed to sermons that use the text to illustrate a theme that may or may not relate to the text) were, like many, Sunday-morning churchgoers. They do not attend an adult class; their own reading of serious Christian books is spasmodic at best. And every church has such folks. Where are they to hear the words that have functioned so prominently in the making of Christian identity if not in and through a sermon? The preaching moment is a teaching moment. No matter how familiar you as a preacher may be with a text, do not assume that your congregation's familiarity equals your own—or even if it does and more, do not assume that your congregation does not yearn for fresh insight into a text.

But if this is what your hearer is listening for, your hearer may discard whatever you say that does not directly feed that desire. Your listener might well be tuning you out or checking mildly for some kind of textual content in your delivery. Of course, the same process might be going on even if you preach a sermon that is closely tied to the text—your hearer will hear you selectively, depending upon his or her needs. You might as well give the sermon away, because you yourself cannot control what your hearer will listen for, let alone what God will do with that sermon in relation to any particular hearer!

Another comment: "I need sermons that help me gain a different perspective on things." In a sense, there is a desire on the part of your hearers that every Sunday should become a kind of a Reorientation Session. We come to church on Sundays immersed in a week that has yielded the usual round of joys and sorrows, problems and triumphs, humdrumness and interest. It's not that we come to church to escape that world—far to the contrary. We come to church in order to worship God in the midst of that world. We bring our worlds with us, and offer them to God—and in the very act of offering, that world is recontextualized in the light of worship. Worship is the opportunity for insight. And insight becomes the simple act of viewing the same situation in a different light.

This insight is gained sometimes because of your preaching, and sometimes in spite of your preaching—it is God, whispering to each person, who can pick up your words and turn them to precisely the symbol needed by your listener to create the act of insight. For example, Joe comes to church still hurting from Mary's rejection of him. It's not only the loss of a possible relationship he suffers, but also the damage to his ego. Is there something wrong with him, that she cannot return his affection? And you, knowing nothing of the situation, preach on John 11. Your theme is resurrection. Lazarus is raised, Mary and Martha rejoice: Life is made new. Joe hears. In the hearing, he looks at his situation as a kind of death—death of a possible relationship, death of certain hopes, and the injury of a shattered ego. And viewing his circumstances under the imagery of the death of Lazarus, he sees his situation as just possibly—by the grace of God's resurrection power—holding within it new possibilities for life, even though he cannot yet envision what these possibilities could be. The pain continues, but the despair is now tinged by a kind of hope. He trusts God with his pain, and also with the birth of hope. God is a God of resurrection power. In the process of your preaching, Joe has gained a new perspective, informed by the gospel, on his life.

But as you preached on John 11, you did so unaware of Joe's need. In fact, what you actually preached was a sermon on answered prayer, based on the fact that Jesus responded to Mary's and Martha's request. The reason behind your choosing such a sermon had to do with your own struggles in prayer, especially as you prayed with the Browns for healing of their critically ill child. John 11 spoke to you of hope and answered prayer. And so you preached.

In the preaching, of course, you re-presented Christ in and through major symbols of Christian faith. Christ's compassion, sorrow turned to joy, resurrection: These were themes included in your sermon. While the Browns might well have heard your sermon relative to their prayers for their child, God turned the symbols into the sermon Joe needed to hear. So when he shakes your hand as he leaves and thanks you for your sermon, he's thanking you for a sermon you didn't know you preached. But you let the sermon go. And God did with it as only God could. You do not know what God will do with what you give. Therefore, you must give your sermon as a "giving away," outcome unknown.

Another response I heard when I asked my friends what they wanted from a sermon was, "I would like, in the preaching moment, to have some sense of God's presence." As preachers, we can shrink back from such a demand—how are *we* to give someone a sense of God's presence? The answer, of course, is that we can't. Nor do we need to. This is God's job. Your job is simply to be faithful in re-presenting what God has done for us in Christ. As you preach, you must be certain that you offer in some configuration that constellation of symbols that God in Christ is for us. There is a story: God created us. For whatever reason (and the Christian tradition names several) there is sin in the world, and we are all embroiled in that sin. God loves, is incarnate, and redeems us in Christ. God is a God of resurrection power; God makes a way for us out of no way; God calls us into communities of caring; God takes creation unto God's own self. Each aspect of the story is conveyed through clusters of images, each of which has the power to suggest the full story. A manger is an image that holds within it the awe of incarnation, the hiddenness of God, the humility of God, the glory of God, the wood of a cross, and the resurrection to come. A star is an image that speaks not only of epiphany, but of revelation, of mercy, of guidance, of providence, of a journey and journey's end in the discovery of Christ. But it's not just these images that convey God's story, God's merciful presence. The very words we use to express the story have power. For example, consider the word epiphany. It suggests the whole paradoxical notion of the manifestation of God in the midst of hiddenness. God is manifest in a small child, manifest in a time of danger, manifest even in a time of flight—and ultimately manifest on a dark cross. The message, then, is that shining underneath every cloud in our lives is the God of presence. One could anticipate, perhaps, that God would be present in the high and glorious times of our lives, but what of that? At such times we might not be particularly in need of the conviction of divine presence! But ephiphany proclaims God's presence even in the midst of things that would obscure God's presence. Epiphany says, "even here, God is present for our good—even here." God is here. Epiphany carries within it the whole hope of the gospel.

As you preach, you give the primary symbols of Christian faith to the people. You do not control the symbols—far from it; they are controlled by a whole galaxy of meaning conveying that God is graciously present to us. The God of Jesus Christ is a God of presence, and the story tells us that God is present to us for our good. That good may entail judgment, comfort, correction, guidance, but this is determined by God, not you. As you faithfully give your people the symbols of Christian faith, you must let your sermon go. Let God take those symbols and work with them, and in the process, the God who is always present may in fact communicate a sense of that presence. But this is beyond your control. It rests with God. So let the sermon go: God will use it as God will, touching some when they need it with a sense of presence.

One more comment: "I would like the sermon to touch my heart and head." You must let the sermon go in full recognition that God will use your word to address the fullness of who your parishioners are. God does not speak only to the head or only to the heart! Remember the process dynamics that I shared with you earlier. Emotion and intellect are deeply intertwined. Every thought has an emotional nuance, which gives power to the thought. And emotions struggle for intellectual interpretation. Head and heart represent the fullness of who we are. Precisely because you must let your sermon go, you should strive to bring intellectual and emotional criteria to your sermon. There is intelligence and emotion in every text given to us in the Word of God. Thus, there should also be intelligence and emotion in every sermon you deliver. Fill your sermon with the best thinking you can muster; probe your own thinking for the emotional content, and make that explicit as well. Weave both together in what God gives you to say, and then let it go.

Let me insert at this point what might be a humbling note. "How many sermons do you remember?" I asked my friends. You will blush to hear the answer—almost none. Yet it may be that this is part of the function of the sermon—it may succeed most when it loses itself in the lives of the hearers. Further, there is a cumulative effect to your sermons that may be more important than any one of your sermons individually.

In the process of your regular preaching, you are giving your congregation the fundamental symbols that in the providence of God become the lens through which your parishioners organize and interpret the meaning of their experiences, and so direct their actions. I have often mused about the peculiarity of one of my fellow parishioners at Metropolitan Memorial Methodist Church in Washington, D.C. This was a justice of the Supreme Court who went to Washington in the '70s as a fairly conservative jurist. But week after week he heard the preaching of Bill Holmes, and Bill was fond of sermons that stressed again and again the ethical commitments involved in being a follower of Jesus. Over the years, the justice changed from being a conservative voice on the court to being one of its most liberal voices. And I couldn't help but wonder if Bill's sermons hadn't had something to do with that. The cumulative effect of sermons is the formation of Christian conscience and consciousness. And so, while we parishioners may not be able to give a total recall to any particular sermon you have preached—not even your very best!—the quiet working of your sermons, faithfully given and faithfully received, results in the shaping of our mind-set, our way of seeing the world in and through Jesus Christ.

I have been giving you metaphysical and practical reasons for my advice to let your sermons go, and in the process I've woven a theological basis or two. Let me further that theological basis through the example of Jesus and his use of parables.

Parables were equivalent in many ways to sermons, and most of Jesus' teachings conveyed to us in the gospel are in parabolic form. Scholars tell us that those few interpretations that occasionally follow a parable in the text, such as the intepreted parable of the sower, may be editorial additions supplementing the remembered words of Jesus. More often, Jesus simply gives a parable—and lets it go.

To see the wisdom of this, look what happens when a parable is interpreted, as in Mark 4 and Matthew 13. The interpretation in both texts is quite detailed. We are given the identity of the seeds who fall beside the road and on rocky places and on thorny ground, and on the good ground. We're told precisely what their worries are, and how these worries and deeds affect the growth of the seed. And there it is: a gift untied, unwrapped, and there to be seen precisely as it is. We know when and how and where to apply the parable. Period. End of story. How many of you have ever interpreted the parable in alternative ways?

But look at the uninterpreted parables of the reign of God that quickly follow upon the interpreted parable of the sower in Matthew 13. They are like enigmas, gifts still wrapped and tied and waiting under the tree. The kingdom of heaven is like a man who sowed good seed in his field, but while he was sleeping his enemies came and sowed weeds in the field. Wheat and tares grow together, but only upon maturity can one identify which is wheat and which are tares. The owner of the field determines to let both grow together, separating them at the harvest, saving the one and burning the other. The next parable compares the kingdom of heaven to a mustard seed—smaller than any other, but sown in a field. When it grows to its full height it is larger than all the other plants. And then the kingdom is like leaven, hid in three pecks of meal, leavening it all.

None of these three parables is interpreted, and the last two of them contain enigmas that call out for interpretation—mustard plants are not larger than all other plants, and leaven is a peculiar image for the reign of God, for leaven was often a metaphor with negative connotations. But Jesus does not address these puzzles. He simply gives the cryptic parables, and let's them go. No application of the parables is made, no definitive explanation is given. It's almost as if each parable forms something like the middle of a sentence, with neither the first part nor the last part supplied. And yet this is appropriate, is it not? We were not on that mountainside listening to Jesus; we do not know what the people brought to their listening. Nor do we know what each did with the parable once received. In the interpreted parable of the sower, one can easily insert oneself into it at just one particular spot and all is clarified; one need trouble oneself no further about the parable and its meaning. But when the parable has the

ambiguity of unfinishedness, like the others, it is not so easily categorized or dismissed. We may not be quite sure how
we fit into its meaning, how its nuances address our own
situation. And precisely because of this element of ambiguity, of "middleness" if you will, the parable bends as the Spirit
wills, touching the hearers—and the readers—in ways they
might not anticipate. In effect, Jesus gives the parable—and
lets it go. The very ambiguity Jesus weaves into the parables
is part of their power. Because they are not interpreted, the
interpretation is left up to us. We cannot so easily assign the
parable to this or that meaning—for it may apply where we
have not yet thought. By letting the parable go, Jesus leaves
it for the Spirit to take where it will.

One of the most powerful sermons I ever heard stopped
before it was finished. The preacher was James Lawson, and
he had come to Wesley Theological Seminary to deliver a
Martin Luther King, Jr., sermon. He preached magnificently,
taking us into the theology of the text with inspiration and
depth. And then, just when I thought he was going to apply
the text to our own situation—he stopped! He simply turned
around, and slowly walked down those spiral stairs from
the pulpit, and without a backward glance returned to his
seat, head bowed. We were stunned! How could he sit down;
he hadn't finished! But of course he had. He had let the sermon go, right there, in the middle of the sentence. And the
Spirit began to do its work, applying that sermon in as many
ways, I suspect, as we who were gathered there had need.

Theologically, then, you must let the sermon go because
there is no way you can finish the sermon. When you pre-
pared this sermon—when you received this sermon—you
yourself were the beginning and ending, and the sermon you
heard and wrote was the middle of your own sentence, as
God applied the meaning to you. When you, in faithfulness,
give the sermon away, you give that middle part. It now be-
longs to the fragments of other sentences, as that word
through which God can weave new sentences and para-
graphs and stories and lives together. Let it go.

And finally, here is a very personal reason for giving the
sermon away, for letting it go. Sometimes you preach well,

and sometimes you don't. You know this. It's not possible under these situations of finitude to preach excellent sermons time after time after time. Sometimes you can be downright mediocre. Sometimes the faces in front of you are like so many masks, and you have no idea whether you are reaching anyone at all—but you have a sinking sensation that in fact you are not. This is not one of your better days, but you have to plod on anyhow until the end of your allotted, and totally interminable, time.

As if that experience weren't enough, there's also a sense in which you can never live up to the text. Haven't you sometimes felt the frustration? When you worked with the text, it really seemed quite wonderful—and as you mused upon it, it grew still more beautiful. You felt your sermon rising from this interaction with the text, and you could hardly wait to preach it. Then Sunday morning came. You did your very best—you preached the text as you thought you yourself heard it, but even as you spoke you knew that your words just weren't coming up to the inspiration you felt. What had been insight and inspiration now feels flat to that behind-the-scenes listener who lurks somewhere inside your head while you are preaching. And you sit down discouraged by what feels to you like an absolute failure—and what, in fact, may really be a failure. You have not lived up to the sermon's potential. And in a sense, you are quite right. You never do live up to a sermon's potential. The text is always more than you can adequately say.

So what do you do? You let the sermon go. You cannot hang on to your success or failure. The sermon, such as it was, is in God's hands—God's quite capable hands. Remember the parable of that small and insignificant mustard seed that grew into a great tree. For all you know, God may take your miserable sermon and find a mustard seed in it for some parishioner's consolation, or conviction, or growth. But here's the good part: Ultimately, it's none of your business what God does with your sermons. It's not necessary that you know all the stories. They don't belong to you, any more than your sermon does.

So let it go.

6

The Sermon as Worship

I go to church on Sunday. On an ordinary Sunday, I wake with the anticipation that this is, indeed, Sunday: It's *church* day. My big decision is whether or not to attend the 9:00 o'clock or the 10:45 service, and most often it's the 10:45. This is the smaller service, and I like its intimacy. When I arrive I greet the folk and take my place in my accustomed seat. We have clear windows at Claremont United Methodist Church, and I sit where I can see the mountains and sky, the wonder of God's creation, and meditate before the service begins.

And then there are the opening hymn and rituals, and the reading of the lectionary. I listen to hear if there is a connection between the texts; often I find one, but I admit to sometimes wondering what the selectors had exactly in mind. I listen as Bob preaches, hearing the text in his words, and opening myself to God in the hearing. God blesses me in the hearing, and I am grateful for my pastor's faithful preaching. And the sermon leads to the prayers of the people. Having received the word, we offer ourselves with our concerns for one another and for the mission of the church in the world to God, who receives our prayer. Bob voices the prayer, but his sensitivity to his congregation is such that he weaves our individual and communal petitions into the prayer that we offer to God through him. Having offered our petitions to God, we then offer our own gifts, carved out from our earnings of the week or month, in support of the mission of the church. And we greet one another. Especially at the smaller service, this is a special act of sharing the peace of God with each other. And we join together in the closing hymn at the recessional, receive the well-saying of the benediction, then all join hands and smile at one another as we sing together, "Blessed be the tie that binds."

My daughters belong to the Lutheran and Episcopal churches, and when I am visiting them I delight in going to church with them. In these communions the time of worship is more intentionally ordered around the liturgy, so that every act within the service, whether by clergy or laity, becomes a way of retelling the story of what God has done for us in Christ, and what we are called upon to do for others as the gracious result of God's actions for us. For example, when the gospel is read, it is brought down to the midst of the congregation for its reading, suggesting a number of things, such as God's incarnation among us; the centrality of the gospel message; and the unity of clergy and laity together under the common gift of the gospel. The Lord's supper, rather than the sermon, serves as the high point of every service, suggesting to us that all things flow toward and from the grace manifested in this meal, and that our worship of God is at the very same time God's nourishment of us for our service in the world, both as individuals and as a corporate body.

But whether within my home church, or a liturgical church, or a free church, I go to church on Sundays, and in these simple rites a deep need in me is met. My soul is lifted up to God, and my life is oriented and reoriented in the refreshment of praising God on a Sunday. This simple service organizes my week and speaks to my deepest sense of meaning.

But sometimes I go to church not to worship, but to preach. Usually it is in a church not my own; sometimes it is not even on a Sunday. And this experience is quite unlike that of my ordinary churchgoing. Indeed, I don't feel as if I'm going to church at all—I feel as if I'm going to work, which I am. I usually have no responsibility for the liturgy, that not often being handed over to guest preachers. But I enter the church with the choir, take my appointed place in the chancel, and all through the liturgical portions leading up to the sermon I am "feeling" the congregation. Do you know what I mean? It sometimes seems to me as if all my antennae are out, stretching to sense the personality of the congregation, the unique "self" that a congregation is.

Once someone described people to me as able to imagine themselves encased in venetian blinds, closing and opening them at will. Well, I don't often feel very much like a venetian blind, but I admit that sometimes when I am sensing the spirit of the congregation, I feel as if I do have such "blinds," and they are wide, wide open, letting in as much as possible.

But whereas in an ordinary attendance at church I am open to the fullness of the liturgy and my fellow parishioners and to the pervasive sense of God, in a preaching-attendance I am far more focused on the congregation.

When it's time for the sermon, I usually have asked to read the sermon text myself, incorporating it into the way I preach the sermon. And the actual act of preaching, of course, is emotionally draining. Sometimes I'm asked to give the pastoral prayer following the sermon, and this, too, is work. On the one hand, all my being is focused on God, but the rest of my being (which in itself is an odd way of calculating how much of us there really is) is totally open to the congregation, so that their needs might flow through me in the voiced offering of their prayers. Following the sermon, or the sermon and the prayer, I sit down, always convinced that I haven't done a bit of justice to the text, and that I've done a dreadful job of it. (When I spoke earlier about letting the sermon go, I was speaking to myself, of course.) So I almost always have to endure some wretched moments of inadequacy before I do what I told you to do, and let the sermon go. And we get to the recessional, and I always think about tripping on my way down the altar steps, but I always manage to walk out upright. And then there is the benediction, and the most interesting part of all, which is looking into the eyes of those who shake my hand following the service. Some eyes, of course, are totally glazed; others are intent—but the hand-shaking always seems to me to be the most interesting aspect of the whole affair.

But have I been to church or have I been to work? And I think it is basically a good deal of work, and quite different from the experience of sitting in the pew on the other side of the pulpit. I suspect it is quite different for those of you who preach week after week to the same congregation—my own experience of going to work instead of going to church may be the experience of an occasional preacher. But, nonetheless, I suggest that functioning as a leader of a congregation in worship is quite different from functioning as a member of a congregation at worship, and I have mused about the theology, practicality, and practice of preaching not as work, but as worship. I think that the hard work of preaching, which on the face of it seems so different from the experience of worshiping God in and through hearing the preached word, can in fact be an act of worship. And when it functions as worship rather than work in the mind and heart of the preacher, I suspect a different experience of worship in the congregation as a whole might also be experienced.

The question, of course, is: What exactly *is* worship? We easily name this Sunday morning event a "worship" service, and by that we generally mean the praise of God. But this, of course, only pushes the question back further: What does it mean to praise God? I turn to two sources, the Psalms, and John Wesley's *A Plain Account of Christian Perfection,* seeking to define worship and then applying this to the act of preaching. Through the Psalms we can understand worship as the offering of our whole selves to God in the context of God's own nature. In Wesley we learn to name worship as the love of God and neighbor.

The beauty of the Psalms is that they probe the depth of all human emotions, and offer those emotions to God. Sometimes it's hard, reading the Psalms, for they take us not only to heights of beauty and inspiration, but also to some of the depths of an ugly vindictiveness. Psalm 137 begins with utter poignancy:

By the rivers of Babylon,
    There we sat down and wept,
    When we remembered Zion.
Upon the willows in the midst of it
We hung our harps.

For there our captors demanded of us songs,
    And our tormentors mirth, saying,
"Sing us one of the songs of Zion."

How could we sing the LORD's song
    In a foreign land?
If I forget you, O Jerusalem,
May my right hand forget her skill,
May my tongue cleave to the roof of my mouth,
If I do not remember you,
If I do not exalt Jerusalem
Above my chief joy.

(Ps. 137:1–6)

We weep with the psalmist, and in his or her mournful words every lament we have ever felt against lost joy, unjust suffering, or yearning for a home lost forever pours into those words! And even when our present time is one of peace and satisfaction, we still resonate with the psalmist, for no human emotion is ever far from us, and we can empathize with the deep sorrow of the human spirit that cries out in the psalm.

But then, alas for our pious sentiments, the psalm continues with memories of the actual destruction of Jerusalem, to which the psalmist finally responds,

O daughter of Babylon, you devastated one,
How blessed will be the one who repays you
With the recompense with which you have repaid us.
How blessed will be the one
    who seizes and dashes your little ones
Against the rock.

(vv. 8–9)

We usually leave this portion out of our liturgies, its vindictiveness not being to our liking. Or we allegorize the sentiments, doing our best with mental somersaults to turn them into more respectable responses to injustice.

But the point is not whether or not we like the repulsive sentiment, but the honesty of the psalm itself. Nothing is hidden from God; nothing is shoved back down beneath the surface for fear that it will damage our reputation in front of God or others should it be displayed. If we resonate to feelings of sorrow in the first portion of the psalm, it's also the case that we can resonate with the cry for vengeance in the second portion. Nothing human is alien to us, and like it or not, polite or not, we have felt those feelings too. We have experienced gut responses of desires for vengeance in moments when others have trespassed upon our supposed privileges or dignity. Like the psalmist, we have desired vengeance—though seldom with so strong a provocation as that experienced by those who sat by those long-ago rivers of Babylon.

What the psalm teaches us is that in the act of worship we come to God as we truly are, lifting the whole of ourselves to God. Our emotions are the deepest and surest part of ourselves; they are the "how" of ourselves, the peculiar particularity of who we are. Worship is lifting ourselves, as we are, to God. And the Psalms take us not simply through the emotions of sorrow and vindictiveness, but through every emotion of human experience. Fear of illness, death, old age? Psalm 71! Thirsting for God in a time of spiritual drought? Psalms 42 and 63! Remorse over sin? Psalms 38 and 51! Marriage and sexual feelings? Psalm 45! Love of nature? Ah, so many psalms extol the wonder of God's creation, but perhaps Psalm 8—or maybe Psalm 65—or perhaps Psalm 149 is the favorite. And those dearest psalms of all, those that speak the praise of God, bring out yet other human feelings. Psalm 98, or 103, or 150! Who can exhaust the feelings lifted up to God in the psalms?

If the entire Psalter be asked what worship is, then I suggest the answer is that worship involves lifting the whole of the self before God. This lifting of the self is offering ourselves as we are, not as we think we should be. Worship is an act of honesty before God; it is being ourselves.

But the last six psalms add to this definition by the astonishing way in which they weave together the praise of God and the nature of God. Psalm 145 begins this rhapsody with the tumbling-out words,

> I will extol Thee, my God, O King;
>> And I will bless Thy name forever and ever.
>> Every day I will bless Thee,

And I will praise Thy name forever and ever.
Great is the Lᴏʀᴅ, and highly to be praised;
And his greatness is unsearchable.

(vv. 1–3)

Soon after this beginning the unfolding of who God is begins: "The Lᴏʀᴅ is gracious and merciful…good to all…sustains all who fall, and raises up all who are bowed down. The eyes of all look to Thee. And Thou dost give them their food in due time. Thou dost open Thy hand, and dost satisfy the desire of every living thing. The Lord is righteous in all ways, … The Lᴏʀᴅ is near…" (vv. 8a, 9a, 14–17, 18a).

In Psalm 146, God is extolled as executing justice for the oppressed, giving food to the hungry, setting the prisoner free, opening the eyes of the blind, raising up those who are bowed down, protecting the strangers, supporting the fatherless and the widow. In Psalm 147, God is the one who provides rain, makes grass to grow, gives to the beast its food, and sends out words and statutes and ordinances to guide us. Psalm 148 becomes a midrash on Genesis 1, calling all being in the order of its creation to praise God, and Psalm 149 continues this with a call to human beings to join this mighty hymn of praise. Psalm 150 is like a final paroxysm of joy as the psalmist calls on us to praise God with every instrument we have ever devised, and then finally, in a total exhaustion of joy, simply says, "Let everything that breathes praise the Lᴏʀᴅ! Praise the Lᴏʀᴅ!"

What these last psalms add to our understanding of worship is that we lift ourselves before God in all the honesty of who we are—but now, in the fullness of who we are before God, we are judged by the very nature of the one before whom we stand. The vindictiveness of Psalm 137 is judged by the mercy and lovingkindness of God's nature. Arrogance is judged by God's own compassion. A self-absorption that cares nothing for those less off than the self is brought up short before the one whose nature is to protect the stranger, support the fatherless and the widow, and raise up those who are bowed down. To worship God is to bring ourselves before God as we are, with all our emotions, and to see ourselves in the light of the nature of the God we worship.

How does such a definition affect a theology of preaching as itself an act of worship, rather than simply an act of the work one is called to do? I suggest that when that work of preaching includes within it some call to honesty on the part of the preacher and the hearers, worship is woven into the work of preaching. When that call to honesty dares to name the so-called negative as well as the so-called positive human emotions, worship is woven into the work of preaching. And when that call to honesty entails a naming of the nature of God as revealed in Jesus Christ for us, then worship is woven into the act of preaching.

This is to say that the preacher not only gives this call, these words, this message, as something for others to hear, but that the preacher him- or herself has sought to experience within the sermon his or her own emotional response. One's feelings are taken into sermon preparation and dealt with in light of the nature of God. Having done this work, the preacher then seeks further for the actual sermon to be preached to the congregation. The actual sermon will incorporate the learnings from one's private wrestling with God in ways appropriate to the needs of the congregation. For example, I have learned the phrase, "inappropriate self-disclosure," from some of my homiletics colleagues at Claremont, which means that the preacher has no right to use the sermon as a way of venting his or her own personal problems in front of the congregation. Rather, having done the private work of hearing God's sermon to the self, the preacher is then responsible for offering to the people their own opportunity to present themselves before God, and to judge themselves as individuals and as a congregation in light of God's nature. Only to the extent that the preacher's own struggles can be helpful to the congregation should they be included in the honesty of the sermon, but in all cases, they are at least background to the sermon. The preacher, like the congregation, has responded to the text, and so the preacher is also participating in worship.

I turn now to John Wesley and his *Plain Account of Christian Perfection* for further illumination on worship. I consider this small book a treasure house of Christian thinking, and not only for those people who call themselves "Methodist."

Like the psalmist, albeit in his own eighteenth-century way, Wesley gives voice to all the vagaries of human nature in this book and also bespeaks on every page something of what he sees to be the nature of God. Thus, this book can illumine our understanding of worship and, therefore, offer an interpretation of how the sermon, too, can be an act not just of work, but of worship.

The sum of Wesley's teaching on perfection is that it is love, "pure love, filling the heart, and governing all the words and actions" (p. 51).[8] This love includes a delight in God, a thankfulness for all things, a rejoicing that is deeper than circumstance, and a desire to serve God. Wesley tellingly elaborates on this, saying that "one of the principal rules of religion is to lose no occasion of serving God. And since [God] is invisible to our eyes, we are to serve [God] in our neighbor, which [God] receives as if done to [Godself] in person, standing visibly before us" (p.103).

The love of God, which necessarily spills over to love of God in neighbor, is no arbitrary definition of perfection for Wesley. In his view, God created us so that we might be the image of God, and the image of God, as intimated on page 69, is that we should use to the glory of God all the powers with which we were created. Now these powers, says Wesley, are emotional, intellectual, and physical (or, in his words, our understanding, our affections, and our body). Thus, we were created so that our various gifts of intellect, emotion, and physicality should be fully developed, and all for the sake of glorifying God.

Sin, of course, interferes with our capacity so to live. But God in Christ redeems us from sin and restores us to the place where, by the mercy of God and the power of God's Spirit working in and with us, we might become that which God created us to be. Our understanding shall develop to its fullest capacity, whatever that capacity might be; our affections shall be honored and honorable, and we shall delight in this created embodiedness as the gift God intended it to be. The direction of all these developments of mind, emotions, and body is toward the love of God. And the love of God, of course, is the mirroring in our own redeemed natures of the very nature of the one who has redeemed us.

For Wesley, as for the psalmist, God's nature is boundless love, and God's boundless love, in turn, is a care for all creation's well-being. So we, being restored by Christ to the place where God's intentions for us might unfold, not only pour out our love to God, but in doing so are involved as well in acts of justice that look to the well-being of all creation.

Clearly, we are still hindered by a variety of finite circumstances—ill health, mistakes in judgment, ignorance, and obstacles of all kinds. But these hindrances do not necessarily render the love of God inoperative, either in reception or expression. Rather, they become the vehicles through which that love flows. The intent toward love, which is itself the work of God's Spirit within us, is like a river that simply flows around the obstacles. Or, as Wesley so aptly says, sometimes we love God "hedged in by outward circumstances." But this is no proof that we have no grace. Like the widow's mite, what may seem small can yet be all we have, and it is worthy.

What, then, is worship? Worship is our responsive love toward God—responsive to God's love for us—which tends toward the fullest and highest development of the loving self, no matter what the obstacles may be, for the sake of service to God through service to others. And how does the work of preaching relate to such a definition of worship? Preaching is itself an act of responsive love toward God that involves the development and use of all our powers, toward the end of serving God's people.

Our preaching encounters obstacles of our own limitations. Maybe we have to struggle to wrap our heads around the text, or to find its theological import, or to know just how to express theology. Or maybe we have physical limitations, such as difficulties of speech or a problem of chronic pain. Finite existence gives us more than enough obstacles! But in the deepest sense, in this context, these are insignificant: God's love can flow through and around those obstacles; we can give our mite, and God can turn it into a mint! By grace, God calls and empowers us to develop ourselves to whatever degree is possible for us—and there always seems to be just one more degree beyond the one we think is the limit! And at whatever stage of development we are, we offer ourselves to God for the sake of service. Preaching is part of the service we render in loving response to God. Preaching is therefore an act of worship.

To view one's preaching as an act of worship unites one in a different way with the congregation. That is, too often the perception is that the people have come to worship God, and clergy have come to help them worship God. Clergy set the context for worship, sometimes in consultation with lay committees and other professionals, sometimes alone. They guide the development of the liturgy, the selection of hymns, the arrangement of the altar. And clergy usually lead us in worship, naming the hymns, having the scriptures read, preaching, praying, and "benedicting" us. Through all this work of leading worship, there is a subtle separation from those who have come to worship. We are divided into worshipers and leaders of worship.

But to view one's leadership as itself responsive love for God, exercised now in this role of leadership, is to place oneself among the congregation one leads, not over it. There is a deep togetherness in the exercise of our various gifts together. And by viewing one's leadership, including preaching, as an act of worship, then God, rather than the clergy, is kept the focus of the worship.

I began these chapters by placing preaching within a process theology of the word, stressing the dynamics of relational existence for understanding what is happening in and through the peculiar act of preaching. Let me conclude by taking these reflections on preaching as an act of worship into the setting of process thought.

God surrounds us in every moment. God is present at our every beginning, in the depths of who we are, with perfect knowledge of who we are and perfect love of who we are. God's love for us reflects God's own nature. That is, God loves us toward our good, and therefore judges that in us which makes for evil. The norm of God's judgment is the awesome reality of God's own nature. In God's love for us, God holds us against the ultimate criterion, which is the love of God. That is, God loves us as judge as well as companion. Or, the God who understands us thoroughly also judges us according to standards of what we might yet become.

God's love is guiding. God loves us toward our good given the situation we are in, moment by moment. We receive from God a nudge toward our best becoming. Our own desires for ill block our reception of that nudge, or lead us to adapt it toward less worthy ends. We have the power to deny God. But since what God offers us is our best, our denial of God's guidance—and God's judgment—is a denial of our own best interest. And, since God's guidance to us is always in the context of communities of well-being, our denial of that which is best for us is at the same time a denial of that which is best for the community. In short, we have the power to sin.

Our freedom is our ability to do what we will with God's guidance. I don't mean to indicate that we stand in an absolutely free fulcrum point of being able to decide for or against God. To the contrary, our own choices in the past and the particular circumstances of a myriad of qualifying events can bend us toward or away from God's guidance. But within all these qualifications and parameters, we have a degree of freedom to respond to God from the depths of our being. We have the capacity to receive that whispered word.

I said that God surrounds us. God is not only in our every momentary beginning, but God also is there to receive what we do with each moment. God receives us. It would take a book or two—or at least several chapters in several books—to work with the process dynamic of what it means to say God receives us in every moment. For now it is sufficient just to state the metaphysical fact that God is the ultimately relational One, who gives guidance to every reality in existence as an act of creativity, and who receives the results into God's own nature. Metaphysically, then, just as God continuously gives gifts to us in the form of guidance, we continuously give God back the gift of what we have done with that guidance. We are surrounded by God.

When I go to church on Sunday morning, I am no more surrounded by God than I am at any other time in the week. Or, to state it positively, I am just as surrounded by God as I am at all times. But in this time, this Sunday, my entering into that service of worship is my own responsive act of acknowledging this God of creative presence. I intentionally place myself in the place of opening myself to this God I love. I know some of the veils of circumstance, the "hedging-ins" of my life that restrict my love, and some of the veils I do not know: I am too used to them even to see them anymore. I don't know myself anywhere near as well as God knows me. But I bring this self I am to that service of worship, opening myself to the God who surrounds me.

And in this openness, things happen for me and for God. In the opening hymn, I name the worthiness of God, the wonder of God, the majesty of God, and in so doing I wake myself up from the familiarity that dulls me to God's greatness. I sing the glory of the one who is at once my judge and savior. While the order of worship varies from congregation to congregation, in my own church we as a congregation are called together after the opening hymn in a "collect" that formally brings us before the God we have praised in collective prayer. Some form of confession is usually included in these opening words of prayer, acknowledging that we have not loved God or neighbor with our whole hearts, and opening ourselves for the honesty of this judgment. And when the choir sings, it names God in song, in an echo of the call of Psalm 150 to use voice and instrument to sing the praise of God. And I hear the text, that ancient writing. "Hear what the Spirit of God is saying to the churches," I whisper within myself, knowing that this saying will have to do with the symbols that form our Christian identity, and thus with the church's growth in grace and service, which is its mission within and beyond its walls.

Into this context, Bob preaches. The textual word becomes an enfleshed word. And God takes the word and applies it to the various conditions of each parishioner, including me, and to the congregation as a whole. In a sense we are washed in that word, and following it we bring ourselves again in prayer to God. The rhythm is appropriate: The preacher offers God's word to us, and then offers our words to God in prayer. God offers guidance to us, and then we offer ourselves in response to that guidance to God. And when we are called upon to give the offering, we are called by God to give from that deeper gift of our whole selves.

So then, having sung God's praises, received God's word, and given ourselves back to God, we greet one another as those always newborn in Christ our Lord. The peace we pass is the peace mediated by this place, this word, this giving and receiving both personally and collectively from and to God. Having done this, we sing once more, but now a song of sending, and we receive the words of good-saying, and leave with lifted hearts.

Do you hear the rhythm of the worship? We receive, we integrate, we give. Worship replicates the creative dynamics of existence itself, only now specifically in relation to the God who creates through call and who receives through Christ. In process thought, worship is our responsive love to God in and through our naming of who God is. And in this naming, we become more open to who God calls us to be. Responsive love responds to God's own love, for God first loved us, and therefore evokes our love in return. Worship is openness to God's gift, integrating God's gift, and giving ourselves back as gift to God in loving service to one another and, optimally, to all God's creatures in this world.

Preaching is also a replication of this rhythm. It is a receiving from God, an integration of the word with a message for the congregation, and a giving of that message in responsive love. Preaching is an act of worship. And preacher and parishioner are woven together in the community that is both gift of God and gift to God in the great rhythm of life. For worship is a sacralization of life, its purification through openness to God and responsiveness to God.

When you preach, then, you fit into this rhythm. Yes, you are leading in worship, but it is more than that: You are a participant in worship. And insofar as you preach, knowing that in so doing you are responding to God in worship, you will know more deeply your own unity with the people of God. Together, we will yet praise God more faithfully in the preaching that is, after all, our whole life's work and worship.

Sermons

I have suggested that the following seven symbols embody Christian faith:

1. The universe as the creation of God
2. The problem of sin
3. The provision of sin's answer in Jesus Christ, who reveals God to us
4. The possibility of new life that triumphs over sin
5. The creation of community
6. The work of God through that community in the world
7. The hope of everlasting redemption

Each of the following seven sermons focuses upon one or more of these symbols.

Creation as Call

Texts: Genesis 1; Psalm 148

The Spirit of God brooding over the face of the waters! What wonderful imagery! It bespeaks a womblike time of darkness, teeming full with all manner of potential things, brimming with hope for that which is not, but which might yet be! The Spirit of God hovers over those waters, and then the wonderful word comes: Let there be Light! And creation begins.

How haunting the majesty of our creation story in Genesis 1. It matters not in this day of evolutionary awareness that the texts speak in mythic tones deeper than any literal history could tell. What matters is the wonder of "isness"— that God created at all, in any way God should choose. God's Spirit broods over the waters!

And what of that parallel creation text, Psalm 148? If Genesis gives an account of creation from the divine point of view, Psalm 148 gives an account of creation from the creature's point of view. Hear the joy of it! "Praise the LORD! Praise the LORD from the heavens; praise God in the heights! Praise God, all angels; praise God, all His hosts! Praise God, sun and moon; praise God, all stars of light! Praise God, highest heavens, and the waters that are above the heavens! Let them praise the name of the LORD, for God commanded and they were created..." The psalm is a paean of joy, as the psalmist matches the order of creation in Genesis 1 with an order of praise in Psalm 148, till the whole universe of creation is united in joy before God.

In reading such creation texts, there is a tendency to relegate such wonders to some dawn of time. And this is surely

Delivered at Baltimore-Washington Annual Conference.

understandable, for Genesis speaks to a beginning of things. But the psalm! Ah, and there's the real wonder of it, for while the psalm parallels the Genesis story, it is presented not as a past joy, but as a present call to joy, along with its joyous response. And yet its context is Genesis 1, the creation: Is that not a long-past thing? The psalm suggests to us that the answer is yes and no: Yes, creation is a long-ago beginning. Don't our physicists speak about billions of years ago as the timing for the beginning of our universe? But the wonder is that what was begun is not an ending to creation, but a beginning of a process that continues to this day. It's not that God *was* creator—God *is* creator! How are we to understand this?

Once a physicist asked me if I would like to see where the "big bang" began. "Sure," said I incredulously—my, how these physicists do taunt one! "Right here," he grinned. Every point in the universe is the point of its beginning. For one who is decidedly *not* a physicist, the statement seems like a conundrum—or more like a profound mystery. Here! Here! *This* is the mysterious spot of beginning! Not some alien, distant place, but here!

Even so, God's creation from the very mists of time is nonetheless in the *midst* of time. Now! Now! Now is the time of God's creating, "as it was in the beginning, is now and ever shall be!" So long as there is a world, God is creating. The very activity of God at the "beginning" is the same activity of God here, now.

But *how* is God creating now, as then? A very practical way to approach it may be to turn to some interesting words that John Wesley preached in that little book that I often quote, *A Plain Account of Christian Perfection*. Smack in the middle of the book, on page 69, Wesley speaks about the creation of Adam. Adam, he says, was "required…to use, to the glory of God, all the powers with which he was created. Now he was created free from any defect, either in his understanding or his affections. His body was then no clog to the mind." What kind of a creation is this? Just as the psalmist bespeaks a responsive creation, singing out the praise of its maker, even so Wesley speaks of a responsive Adam. But the Wesleyan take on Adam's responsiveness is particularly instructive. God, in creating Adam, required Adam to use that which had been given to him. And this applied not simply to one aspect of himself, such as his mind. Rather, Adam was to use *all* the powers with which he was created to the glory of God. Mind, affections, body—all were to be developed to the fullest, and in this development, God the creator would be glorified.

The implication, surely, is that God creates a creature full of potentiality, and that God calls the creature itself to develop that potentiality. And now go back to that Genesis text. God broods over the waters and calls out the command: "Let there be…!" And at the command of God, the waters move, respond, and it happens! There is light, there are the heavens, the sun, the stars, the earth, its creatures! God creates through call and response! In Genesis the response is existence, and in the Psalms the response is praise. In its very responsiveness, creation occurs, and the creation is itself the praise of God.

Is it not the case that God is always creator? And always creating? Is it any different today? Return now to the Wesley text. God creates humans with all sorts of wonderful powers—powers of intellect, of affection, of body. And throughout our entire lives God is brooding over us, calling us to the fullness of who we might be. God calls us to develop our minds, to think and probe and wonder and guess, learning and teaching all the while! God calls us to develop our affections, most specifically developing the capacity to love with the whole of who we are, to the glory of God. And God calls us to develop these marvelous bodies we are, to whatever capacity is possible for us. And in the integration of mind, affections, and body we become who we are called to be. As we do so, our creator is glorified.

Is there a restlessness in you to think more deeply, to struggle to formulate more clearly the faith that is within you? The creation accounts suggest that this is God, brooding over you, calling you through that very restlessness. Dare to go beyond where you are now, dare to think, dare to learn, dare to teach! And as you respond to the call to develop the fullness of your intellectual capacities, your very being can become the praise of God.

Is there a yearning in you to open yourself more fully to love? Do you fear such a thing, as if to do so opens you as well to a terrible vulnerability? You are correct, for to love is indeed to be vulnerable, but it is the vulnerability of life itself, and it is for the glory of God. Dare to open yourself fully to the risk of loving, developing your affectional life to the fullest. And do not let your love be narrowly restricted, but dare to open your heart to caring in increasingly wider circles of love. Let your loving reach beyond your own circle to embrace a care for the well-being of those who differ from you; let your love reach beyond your familiar friends to touch the stranger in need; let your love caress this world of trees and grass and hills and valleys, seeing to its well-being! Oh, respond to the call to develop your love to its fullest, and you will be the praise of God.

Nor should you despise this physical stuff that we are, as if it were not also part of the very creation of God. Rejoice in this physicality, whatever its condition, and know it to be the gift of God. Look to your care of your physical self, whether you are in the vibrancy of youthful health, the steady sturdiness of middle years, or the fullness of many years. There is an optimum for you that suits your very own condition, whether that condition be "hedged in by outward circumstances" of illness or disability or not. There is a best for you! Live responsively into all the goodness of what it is to be embodied, for you are the creation of God. And in your responsive care, you participate with God in creation through your own fuller development of yourself.

God creates by calling us into being. The amazing graciousness of God's manner of creating is that our own responsiveness is part of the creative activity ordained by God. God did not create us as passive, but as active respondents, so that in and through our answer to God, creation continues.

Through Wesley, I have spoken of each of us individually as God's creation. But the psalm takes us into the deeper reality in its echo of Genesis 1, for the psalm names all of creation, whether animate or inanimate, in whatever stage of existence it may be, to be in union. There is a deep connectedness weaving through us all, and that connectedness is in and through God who has called us individually and together into being and becoming. We are, together, called to be a great choir in concert with the whole universe, singing the praise of God. And our singing is our very being, our joyful responsiveness that is our co-laboring with God as we, by God's design, participate in our own creation.

There is more to the story, of course. There are our failures to respond to God's creative call, and that becomes the counterpoint story of sin and egregious evil. But God's creative call comes yet again in the provision of sin's answer in Jesus Christ. Christ restores us to the place of good responsiveness once again.

So then, God is creator of all that is. And God's mode of creating is by calling us into being—not just once, but again and again and again, so long as creation shall last. We in this moment of time take up our own part in the creation story. Rejoice! Respond to God's call! Be fully who you can be, individually and together, doing the creative work of God in this world. The Spirit broods; the Spirit calls; creation is happening here, now! Let us respond, and praise the Lord!

The Welcoming God

Text: Ephesians 1–3

It's not the first time there's been controversy in the church! For as long as the church has existed, there is evidence of controversy and resolution that left both joy and dissatisfaction in its wake. The beauty of the New Testament is that it records such times, which I consider to be a unique gift of the Spirit. For if all the New Testament ever recorded were times of ideal unity, then where would be its guidance for today? Or where would be the encouragement that, just as we see the Spirit working in the controversies of those times, we can also trust the Spirit to be working in the controversies of our own times?

So this morning we look at one of those biblical controversies in order to learn something of the Spirit's work then. Seeing it then, we might also discern that same Spirit now. The controversy I have in mind is the controversy over just how inclusive the early church would be. Indeed, the one time of unqualified harmony that we see in New Testament times is in those first pages of the book of Acts, where the newly converted Christians had all things in common, met regularly in one another's homes for eucharist, and took their meals together with gladness and sincerity of heart. But of course those were the days when all the Christians were Jews who were also Christians. They were a homogeneous community who had not yet been tested by the real challenge of diversity that was to come.

And when it came! It nearly split the infant community

The context for this sermon was the California-Pacific Annual Conference of the United Methodist Church at a time when the Conference was embroiled in hostile divisions within itself over approaches to the issue of homosexuality. The Conference was considering a consensus model toward the end of being a "Welcoming" Conference.

wide apart! For it was quite clear that this new notion of inclusiveness was quite against the biblical witness. Didn't the scriptures clearly give God's word that to be a member of the covenant meant to be a circumcised keeper of the law of Moses? And it wasn't Moses who gave the command, but God's own self! Surely God wouldn't change the divine mind over so serious a thing as the sign of the covenant! If it says in Holy Scripture that males should be circumcised as a sign of God's holy covenant, then they should be, and that settles it!

Gentiles would be welcomed into the congregations, indeed they would, but welcomed as God-fearers, even as they had been in the Jewish synagogues. They couldn't be *full* Christians, any more than they could be full Jews, without circumcision! Oh, indeed, there were rumblings here and there in the sacred text of Isaiah about the Gentiles coming to the Lord not by circumcision, but through learning from the Jews the ways of justice and mercy. But anyone could plainly see that most texts indicated that in order to be full members of the covenant, acceptable to God, Gentiles were required to keep the full law of Moses, even as Jewish Christians did.

But there were troubling signs. There was that business about Peter and Cornelius, and there was gossip that Paul was telling even Jewish Christians that they need not have their sons circumcised. The controversies swirled. Then, in Acts 15, there is the account of an Annual Conference in Jerusalem (they called them councils in those days) and the long discussions of pro and con: Should Gentile Christians be accepted within the community, even if they were not circumcised? Shouldn't they rather submit to the clear word of God and accept the holy sign of the covenant? If they were not circumcised, were they not still sinners, outside the covenant? The questions were not easy, but finally the Council decided by consensus that the Gentiles should be welcomed, with the only constraint being that they refrain from sacrificing to idols, and that they live lives of sexual faithfulness rather than promiscuity. The church, in and through its intense controversy, decided on this new thing: They should be a welcoming church.

Now one would think this would settle it, but that great letter to the Ephesians shows that it wasn't settled quite as nicely as one would hope. Indeed, even the book of Acts shows the controversy immediately following that Council, for Paul and Silas have a falling-out over whether or not to include John Mark again in the missionary journey. The text doesn't tell us why John Mark left them so precipitously back in Pamphylia, but one could wonder whether it might not have had something to do with this controversy over Paul's not requiring the Gentiles to obey the law. But in any case, Paul won't go through that again, so Paul and Barnabas split up—Barnabas takes Mark and goes off in one direction, and Paul takes Silas in yet another.

But what of that book of Ephesians? Because that particular controversy is so far removed from us, we sometimes fail to realize the astounding nature of this epistle, for it gives insight into how the writer speaks to those who were second-class citizens in the church. There were the Jewish Christians who had received the sign of the covenant—and then there were those Gentile Christians, who had not. How were they to be one church?

The points to notice are that first and foremost, the Spirit works in controversy by lifting our minds and hearts to wonder at the awesome goodness and mercy of God. The point of the book is that God in Christ working through the Spirit has broken down the wall of hostility between Jewish Christians and Gentile Christians. Furthermore, God has intended from all eternity that this wall shall be broken down, and accomplished it in and through the resurrection and ascension of Jesus Christ. But the writer doesn't really get to this until the middle of chapter two. The entirety of chapter one is devoted to the praise of God, who in lavish grace has accepted us. In justice and mercy God has chosen from all eternity to welcome us, to accept us, and even more, to adopt us. Hear the words that speak of the lavishness of God!

> In love God predestined us...according to the kind intention of God's will, to the praise of the glory of God's grace which God freely bestowed on us in the Beloved...

> In Christ Jesus we have redemption through his
> blood, the forgiveness of our trespasses, according to
> the riches of God's grace which he lavished upon
> us…In him also we have obtained an inheritance…to
> the end that we who were first to hope in Christ [the
> Jewish Christians] should be to the praise of his glory.
> In him you also [the Gentile Christians], after listening
> to the message of truth, the gospel of your salvation—
> having also believed, you were sealed in him with
> the Holy Spirit of promise, who is given as a pledge
> of our inheritance, with a view to the redemption of
> God's own possession, to the praise of his glory…I
> pray that the eyes of your heart may be enlightened,
> so that you may know what is the hope of his calling,
> what are the riches of the glory of his inheritance in
> the saints, and what is the surpassing greatness of
> his power toward us who believe.
> (Ephesians 1:5–7,11a,12–14,18–19)

And is this not instructive for us? For we come together
to discern God's will, even if that will is not what we expect.
And what we see as we look for God's leading is even greater
than the leading—it is the vision of the boundless graciousness of the God who redeems us in Jesus Christ. Welcoming!
We have each of us, sinners all, been welcomed by God, the
God of creation and redemption and sanctification, which
should cause us to bow in tearful humility at such wondrous
grace.

Chapter one concludes with reference to the resurrection
and ascension of Jesus Christ, and that theme is picked up
again in chapter two. The surpassing greatness of God's
power toward us who believe is precisely the power that was
at work in the resurrection of Jesus Christ—it is resurrection
power, which we, who were dead in trespasses and sins,
surely need! We walked according to the power of this world,
which is a power for destruction, not resurrection. Power, as
we are too grimly aware, is measured in this world by the
ability to destroy those with whom we disagree. Power is in
the tossing of the head over the nuclear capability to uncreate
God's world, beginning with those we call enemy. Power is

in the despising of those with whom we disagree. The world's power is the opposite of resurrection; it is murderous will; it is destruction; it is sin; it is death. And such were we. But God! God *is* the power of resurrection, of life; God is "rich in mercy" because "even when we were dead in our transgressions [God] made us alive together with Christ and raised us up with him and seated us with him in the heavenly places, in Christ Jesus!"

Do you see it? We live in resurrection power! Knowing this, our controversies are to be measured by the will toward life, not the will toward death! Our disagreements are in a deep sense the opportunity for the power of the resurrection to be at work in us, showing the world against its hungry power of death that there is a deeper power at work. Because we are in Christ, we can extend a will for life and well-being toward those with whom we disagree! Ah, they shall know we are Christians by our love, and our love is witness to the resurrection power of God that is in Christ *and* (oh, by grace we are saved!) in us.

Finally in chapter 2 we have the culmination, the "so what" of everything the writer has said. *Therefore!* Because of this resurrection power, because of this welcoming God, even while we are different, even though we remain circumcised Jewish Christians or uncircumcised Gentile Christians, there is no wall of hostility between us! For Christ is our peace—the resurrected Christ who brings us into his resurrection—he himself, working through the Spirit, abolishes in his flesh all causes for our enmity, our alienness, our marginality. He himself is our peace who made both groups—Gentile Christians and Jewish Christians—into one, reconciling both in one body to God through the cross, leading both into lives transformed by the love of God and one another, which is the peace of God.

Do you suppose that it is God's own design that we should have controversies, in order that we might be a witness to the world of how resurrection power deals with controversy? Do you suppose that God calls us as a church to tell the nuclear arms–waving spirit of this world that there is a lavishness of grace and a richness of mercy to build up, not tear down? Will they know we are Christians by our love?

For through Christ both Gentile Christians and Jewish Christians, both reconciling Christians and transforming Christians, both heterosexual Christians and homosexual Christians, both consensus Christians and respectful dissident Christians, have access in one Spirit to God. "And we are no longer strangers and aliens, but we are fellow citizens with the saints, and are of God's household, having been built upon the foundation of the apostles and prophets, Christ Jesus being the chief corner stone, in whom the whole building, being fitted together is growing into a holy temple in the Lord, in whom we also are being built together into a dwelling of God in the Spirit." We have been welcomed by God into God's own household! Oh, let us then be welcoming of one another!

Good Friday Meditation

Text: John 19:28, "I am thirsty," and John 19:30, "It is finished!"

I remember singing in a choir the staccato sarcasm of Matthew 27:41 and 42 in *The Seven Last Words of Christ*, by DuBois: "*If* thou be Jesus, *son* of the father, *down* from the cross descend thou—that we may *see* thee and be*lieve* up*on* thee." We were to sing it sharply, with derision, and to sing it thus was to feel the centuries of cruel mockery not only against the Christ, but against us who hold that in this One on that cross, we do indeed see God.

And the mockery is age-old, coming seemingly from opposite directions. There were the Docetists in the early church who claimed that God was metaphysically incapable of being on that cross, for how could the majestic God of all the universe be so humbled as to experience this most ignoble and worst of deaths? And so, they said, Christ had only the appearance of us real human beings, not our substance, and it was but the appearance that suffered there on that awful cross. God is not there!

And then there were and are the moralists who claimed that God could not be on that cross, for God almighty is incapable of identifying with the sin that was represented on that cross. Rather, God had turned away, and what we see on the cross is not the presence of God, but the wrath of God. God, present in the innocent Christ, separates from the sin-laden Christ, and in that terrible parting shows the full force of God's hatred of sin. Far be it from God to feel that sin! No, God is not there!

Preached at Claremont United Methodist Church.

Secularists, too, join the chorus of this text, mocking the very thought that the man on that cross is anything other than a man very much in trouble. But God? What fanciful naivete could dream up such a fairy-tale belief! God is not there!

The gospel text in John gives the answer: "**I am thirsty.**"

But let me say it again, this way: The gospel text in **John** gives the answer, "I am thirsty."It is in John that we find this particular word of dereliction; John! Do you not remember? For the gospel of John is the very book that dares to build on the Exodus passage, "I AM THAT I AM," with the "I am" statements of Jesus! In Exodus, Moses has asked for God's name, knowing that in God's name is God's power. If Moses but knew God's name, Moses would know God. But the only name given to Moses from out of that blazing fire was the enigmatic "I AM," with no predicate provided. There is no description of God, merely the "I AM" of God.

The wonder of this gospel of John is that here we see Jesus as the very predicate of God. It is as if Jesus fills in the blanks of God, providing finally the meaning of that great "I AM." Don't you remember how they tumble out, chapter after chapter? In chapter six, Jesus claims "I AM THE BREAD OF LIFE. Whoever comes to me will never be hungry, and whoever believes in me will never be thirsty," and again, "I AM THE LIVING BREAD that came down from heaven...and the bread that I will give for the life of the world is my flesh." In chapter 8 it is "I AM THE LIGHT OF THE WORLD." And in case we don't "get it," chapter 8 then concludes with Jesus saying, "Very truly, I tell you, before Abraham was, I AM." The "I am's" of Jesus in the gospel of John are the revelation of who God is; Jesus is the predicate of God.

In chapter 10 we hear, "I AM THE GATE. Whoever enters by me will be saved," and again, "I AM THE GOOD SHEPHERD. The good shepherd lays down his life for the sheep," which is closely followed by "The Father and I are one." Chapter 11 gives us the astonishing "I AM THE RESURRECTION AND THE LIFE," and in chapter 14, "I AM THE WAY, THE TRUTH AND THE LIFE." In John 15 we are given the precious "I AM THE VINE, you are the branches!"

Too often we have thought of this image of the vine as the last "I AM" statement, but look, look, there is one more! And it is one to break your heart, for all these nouns that announce the all-sufficiency of God for us finally culminate in an adjective crying out the pain of God for us, "I am thirsty."

What can this mean?

Against the Docetists who say that a great metaphysical gulf exists between God and ourselves, the "I am thirsty" renders that gulf void. God is there in the very midst of physical suffering, sharing our suffering, tasting our suffering. In our thirst, God is also thirsty. God is there!

Against the moralists who say God could not bear even to look on the sin of the cross, "I am thirsty" reveals a God not simply present to the suffering of physical pain, but to the suffering of sin. It is God who feels with us our thirst after righteousness; it is God who experiences with us the agony of our sin in all its bitter effects in this world. God is there!

And the secularists might yet say, So what? What is the good of a God who thirsts in our thirsts, suffers in our pains, agonizes in our sins? Is God no better than we are, that God should be so drastically affected by our suffering? What kind of a God is this!

But hear the good news of the gospel. It is God's very presence with us in our pain that makes it possible for God to bring forth for us forms of our own transformation, forms of resurrection in this life as well as in the next. If God were a distant God, removed from our suffering, how would God know our deepest needs in any but an abstract way? But no! The "I am thirsty" reveals that God is not absent from us in our deepest need; God knows us feelingly! And the mystery is that precisely because God knows us feelingly, God can feel for us our own mode of resurrection, our own transformation that yet renders this Friday good. It is God's Friday indeed. God is there.

God's suffering with us is God's own means of raising us again. God is on that cross. God is in Christ, reconciling the world to Godself. The great "I AM" of God receives its deepest meaning as God's majesty is shown, finally, to be God's mercy. God is there.

And so the revelatory "I am thirsty" is followed with the factual "It is finished." It is sufficient. God in Christ knows us fully; God in Christ therefore redeems us fully. God identifies with our crucifixions in order that we might identify with God's resurrections. It is finished: New life begins.

"If thou be Jesus, son of the father, down from the cross descend thou, that we may see thee and believe upon thee," becomes, in the gospel of God's Grace,

> Because thou art Jesus,
> Son of the Father,
> You tasted our pains—
> Our pains to the depths.
> You drank of our vinegar,
> Our most bitter sorrow.
> And thus made a way for our own
> Participation
> In your Easter.
> And yes, yes!
> Oh yes!
> We do believe upon thee!

It is finished indeed; and our Easter is ever before us. Amen.

The First Breakfast

Text: John 21:1–22

Don't you hear the echoes in this passage? It's such a dearly familiar story! The disciples, on the Sea of Galilee, fishing all night with no luck at all, until Jesus appears and tells them where to cast their nets! And Peter recognizes him, and swims toward him. The disciples soon follow in the boat, hindered a bit by a net so heavy with fish that the nets almost break! They hesitantly come to that breakfast table to eat bread and fish with their now risen Lord. And then the awful asking: Peter, do you love me? Do you love me? Do you love me? And the agonized answer, thrice given, yes, oh yes, oh you know that I do! The text doesn't have to tell us why Jesus asks three times, forcing Peter to answer three times! We hear its original in the echo; we know that the three-fold betrayal is now answered by a threefold affirmation.

After all, it's not so strange. Each of us has at some time or other experienced the hard betrayal of love, whether against us or by us. We have let down a friend; we have broken a vow; we have disillusioned a child! But the deeper reality of love will not rest with those betrayals; betrayal must finally be overturned in renewed affirmations of faithfulness. "Simon…[not now Peter, the rock, but that earlier pre-Jesus name]…son of John, do you love me more than these," repeated three times, is the inverse of those voices in the night saying, "Surely you were with him!" And the answering cry, "Yes, Lord, you know that I love you!" is the final denunciation of the betrayal. We hear the echo, and know the triumph! In it, Simon becomes Peter again, renewed in Christ's own resurrection power.

Delivered at Trinity Lutheran Church, Redondo Beach, California.

But it's not the only echo in the text. We readily understand this echo, but see, there are three others that precede it! We hardly notice them, perhaps because while each bit of a story is indeed an echo of an earlier story, it's told now with a particular difference that disguises its echo-form. Look at them, and ask: Why the difference? Why is it not a direct parallel, like Peter's reversal of his former betrayal?

Remember the original of the first echo that occurs in the opening verses of this chapter? The disciples, bereft of Jesus, go to the Sea of Galilee. Simon announces that he is going fishing, and the others say, "We'll go with you." So they fish all night, catching nothing till the break of day, when the unrecognized Jesus appears on the beach. "Cast the net on the right-hand side of the boat," says he, "and you will find a catch." And indeed, the catch is such that the nets are full, close to bursting, but "although there were so many, yet the net was not torn."

Remember where you first found that story? Luke puts it not at the end of his gospel, but at the beginning, in the calling of the disciples recounted in chapter 5. It's not surprising that the story should be placed differently, for we know that these gospels were written decades after the events they record. For years and years the church lived from its oral tradition as the stories were told again and again, story by story, heart by heart! When these gospels were compiled, the stories were strung together like beads on a string, with one writer putting the story here, and another, the story there! And so Luke puts the story at the beginning, while John puts the story—like an echo—at the end.

How does Luke tell the story? Simon, James, and John had been fishing all night without success; they are washing their barren nets in the morning when Jesus comes by, and uses Simon's boat as his pulpit! He teaches the crowds, and when he is finished, he tells these fishermen to go back out to sea and to let down their nets. And when they do, they bring up such a catch that the nets begin to break, and even the boats to sink under so great a catch! Astonished, they come ashore and bow before Jesus, who tells them to follow him!

The story is almost exact, even to the "Follow me!" that concludes the story in John, except for one seemingly insignificant detail. In Luke, the catch is so great that the nets break. But in John, even while the catch is very great, the nets do not break. As if to emphasize the point that the nets could well have been expected to break under so great a catch, John even tells us how many fish there were—one hundred and fifty three, and very big ones at that! But the nets do not break. Why this difference?

The next echoed story is buried in the midst of this first one. It's the story of Peter leaping into the sea when he knows it is, indeed, the Lord! And he swims to him! Is it too fanciful to see here an echo of that earlier story when, in the gospel of Matthew, the disciples are alone in a boat in the fourth watch of the night, which was toward morning? And suddenly they see a figure which they take to be a ghost, walking toward them on the waves. When he speaks, they know it to be the Lord, and Peter leaps over the boat to walk toward him, also on the water! Then, as the wind rises, he becomes afraid, and sinks, crying out, "Lord, help me!" Jesus, taking him by the hand, raises him up. So in Matthew, Peter, in the boat, gets out to walk on water toward Jesus; in John, Peter, in the boat, gets out to swim to Jesus. Why this difference?

The third echo may give us the answer. For the disciples come to their Lord, who is already there cooking fish before they bring that which they have caught. Can't you see that scene on the beach, with Jesus stooping over the fire, broiling the fish, waiting for the disciples to come? And come they do, in answer to his invitation! They are overawed by this, and none dare ask him, "Who are you?" for they know it is the Lord. And then there is the recognizable act: He takes the bread, and gives it to them, and the fish likewise. Ah, do you hear the echo? Where else did you hear, "And he took the bread, and gave it to them"? "This is my body, broken for you." But now it's no longer the Last Supper—and in John's gospel, unlike the other three, there is no "Last Supper." For John, the significance of that supper prior to the crucifixion is not the breaking of the bread, but the washing of the disciples' feet, and the great discourse of comfort: "Let not your heart be troubled, neither let it be afraid." He does not lift up the breaking of bread at a last supper; rather, he lifts up the breaking of bread at a First Breakfast! It's no longer the eve of the crucifixion—it's the morning of the resurrection!

Let me interrupt this narrative with quite a different narrative of my own that may cast light on this breakfast scene, and these echoes-with-a-difference. When my little grandson, Mike, was two years old, he and his older sister and his mom and dad would come to spend a weekend with me. Mike and Alexandra slept on the sleeper-sofa in the guest room. Now I hate to tell you, but one of the very special things about Saturdays for me is that there is no alarm clock going off at 7:00 a.m., informing me that it is time to be about the day's work! Not on Saturday! On Saturday, I actually get to sleep until I wake on my own—unless it was those weekends when Mike was there to visit. I'll remember it laughingly as long as I live; along about 6:00 a.m., my sleeping ears would invariably hear this little piping voice saying, "It's morning-time!" And I would open my sleepy eyes to see his smiling toddler face, eyes bright with anticipation, and hands held up to me, telling me the wonderful news: "It's morning-time!" And in those words was all the wonder that once again there was a whole day ahead; once again the miracle had occurred; once again there were wonders to come! Get up! Oh, let's not waste a minute of it! It's morning-time!

And isn't that the message of this First Breakfast? The resurrection of Jesus Christ makes it morning-time! No matter how many years and decades and centuries and millennia have gone by, it's still morning-time! To be in Christ is to live always in the morning-time of this gospel, this resurrection.

And that's why it's a breakfast, and no longer a supper. And that's why the nets don't break, and why Peter swims instead of attempting again to walk. That's why betrayal turns to love renewed, and trust. And that's why the text ends again with the enticing words, "Follow me."

It's breakfast instead of supper because now there's a day ahead, and a work to do, and a mission to accomplish. The reign of God has dawned in Christ, and we are invited into that new day. By God's grace, in Christ's resurrection power we are made co-laborers with God for the work of God.

The nets don't break because now all that's needed is ready; the tools for our work will hold. Before, at the beginning of Christ's ministry, our tools weren't strong enough, but with the full revelation of God for us in the crucifixion and resurrection of Christ, the tools are made ready: The nets are strong, and they will not break. There is work to do, hard work to do, but we are equipped for that work!

And that's why Peter puts off a garment, and swims in the natural strength God gave him. He was a fisherman, he was a swimmer back in Matthew's gospel, but he didn't trust his own strength then! But now he can; it's the morning-time of resurrection! He doesn't have to "walk on water"; he doesn't have to be some superman. In Christ he can be himself; in Christ he is equipped to do the work he is given to do with the nets of the gospel, and it is sufficient!

Is there a work that you as a church have to do? Is there a mission given particularly to you? Your bulletin says that each of you is called to be a minister, serving the needs of those in the community around you, and you can do it! You don't have to be superfolk; you have the wits and strength of your very own selves and are God-graced already for the task! Are your gospel-nets acts of kindness in making a place for neighborhood children to come and be safe? Are your nets acts of mercy in addressing the needs you identify in your community? Are your nets your care for one another as you rejoice in each other's gladnesses, and share in each other's sorrows? Are your nets the way you bear one another's burdens and so fulfill the law of Christ? Pick up your nets and use your strength for the good tasks God gives you; seek out the peculiar work given to you as this special community, and go to it! Your nets are strong enough, and they will not break!

And do not fear that you are unworthy for the tasks before you. The crucifixion is over, and you are invited to renew your love; it's resurrection that bears you up! By Christ you are made a participant in that resurrection, and it's still

happening! You, like Peter, are clothed in Christ's own worthiness. It's morning-time!

This morning you will gather around this table to par-
take in an echo of that Last Supper. You will take bread, and
eat. But as you take and eat that precious bread, remember
that the supper is also a breakfast; the night is always over;
and the bread is to strengthen you for the work of this day.
Christ is risen!

It's morning-time.

Multiplication Tables

Text: Mark 6:32–44

One of the dearest aspects of my life is the joy that I am grandmother to seven children—six grandsons and one granddaughter. Three are in Dallas, two are in Hawaii, and two are close by in Hermosa Beach. I see my distant children as often as I can, and several years ago I had occasion to spend some weeks in the winter with my Dallas children. Later in the spring, I received a letter from Cathy to warm any grandmother's heart. She sent me a homework assignment that seven-year-old Graham had brought home from school. It was an essay on "The Most Important Woman in My Life." I present to you a portion of this remarkable document!

> The most important woman in my life is Marjorie Suchoke...She has spent over 100 dollars on airplans. But she has fun on airplans. But she comes from Calafornya to Dallas. And helps me to learn German words like lihulebadith, wich means I love you. And she taught me how to add and subtrackt and she showd me how to tell time and showd me how to do multiclation tables like 10 x 10 = 100 [spelling original!].

I well remember the drive on a rainy winter day, repeating the sing-song rhythms of those multiplication tables. Little did I know that it was important enough to that small boy that months later he would cite it on his English assignment. Multiplication tables indeed! What he had given me in return

Delivered at Claremont School of Theology's Baccalaureate Communion Service. Note: The breads brought to the table at this communion service represented the staple food of the peoples of the world: rice cakes, poi, corn bread, tacos, pita bread, rainbow bread, and many others.

was the multiplication of love, given and received and given back again one hundredfold.

Our scripture text speaks of multiplication tables of a somewhat different sort. Jesus and the disciples were in a lonely place—but droves of folk sought them out to hear the teaching that Jesus would give. Often the texts tell us of people seeking Jesus for healing, but in this text they seek him for his teaching, and what teaching he gave! Some parallel passages say they stayed in that place for three days, listening to a seminar the likes of which none of us has yet experienced! Out of his compassion he taught them—and is it too fanciful for me to think that he taught them many ways of living out "I love you" to those who gathered there? Oh, not in German, or English, or Korean, or even Hebrew or Aramaic, but in the manner of being with one another, of being community together, of living the words. He taught them! And then the old story of their hunger, and his gathering up seven loaves of bread and two fish, and blessing them…and blessing them…and blessing them…and blessing them…, continuously giving the broken pieces to the disciples who distributed first the bread, and then the fish, till all not only ate, but were satisfied. And when they were finished, there were twelve full baskets left and gathered yet again. And there were 5,000 who ate this bread. What a multiplication upon that mountain table!

We hear the familiar story, but I suggest to you this evening that we participate in this story most deeply on this eve of commencement, here at this table in this place. Think of it, you who graduate tomorrow. Did you not come to Claremont as to a lonely place? Three—four—or more years ago you came not yet knowing this community, these classmates, these teachers. You came to a place strange to you. But you came from a lonely place, too. You came for the teaching, to learn all you could for a ministry to which you were called. Do you remember the hunger that drove you here?

Were you hungry to learn how God speaks to us today? Did you come to open this book, hungry to learn its contents and its meaning? Did you come with nervousness as you began to read the great theologians of the church and began to formulate your own theology of how God works with us and for what end? Did you long to know how to serve the people of God, how to lead others in worship and sacrament, how to preach the gospel, how to care for souls, how to lead the community in faithfulness? If you came in hunger, there was bread for you here as you studied and learned with your professors and classmates. Multiplication tables! For as fast as you thought you had a subject figured out it opened up for you again, revealing further depths, and finally you reach this graduation point knowing you have just begun to learn. In the wisdom of God, knowledge is inexhaustible, and only those who know little think they have learned enough. God spreads a feast before you of bread broken and distributed and gathered to be given yet again, and your whole life will be the adventure of continuing to eat at this table!

But you would be ill-served if the only bread given you was knowledge of who we are and where we are called to be. Your hunger was also of the spirit, for the sense of God's presence is never exhausted, always calling us deeper. For how shall you plumb the depths of the mystery of God? When will you measure the love of God, proclaiming "this much" and no more?

Years ago I learned a love lesson. It was when I was expecting my second child. How dreadfully distressed I was, for I had been loving my little Cathy for two years already, and how could this second child possibly catch up on two years' lead time of love? And I grieved the loss to my child-to-come, whom I considered with impeccable logic always to be in the catch-up position of love. And then she was born, and how I laughed to learn the reality! Love multiplies! It multiplies! It isn't quantitative, so that this one has this much and that one that much—each had 100 percent, and there was 100 percent more for the third! And if a mere mother experienced the joy of such multiplied love, what must it be for a God of infinite love? Ah, there is bread for you to nourish your souls through the infinite multiplication of God's love! Did you know that before you came? Did you deepen that knowledge here? Oh, spend your lifetime learning that there is bread enough, and yet more left over!

Tonight you see a metaphor of your experience. Bread is brought to this table—bread representing all the countries of students gathered here, bread representing us and our coming together in this place. And on this table the bread will be blessed and broken, just as it was on that mountainside so long ago. And there will be enough for all of us to eat, and yet more left over that we gather together once again. You will be satisfied.

But as you leave this table, and tomorrow leave this place, remember the bread that you ate here. Take this bread with you—BE this bread as you leave. And you will encounter people who are hungry. Some will be hungry for the nourishment of physical bread, and you will multiply the skills you learned in this place to help communities organize, some finding work and all finding a way to share their bread with others. Be bread multiplied for those who are hungry!

You will encounter those who hunger and thirst for righteousness. They will long for justice in our world, for our world, they will thirst for righteousness to flow down in our cities and nation and world and earth like an ever-flowing stream! You have learned of God's righteousness; multiply your learning, work with others in community, inspire communities to seek out the ways of righteousness and justice. Feed those who hunger and thirst for righteousness!

And you will encounter those who hunger for God, echoing your own hunger. How do you multiply your learning of the love of God; how do you feed folk with the love of God; how do you awaken folk to the wonder and marvel and joy of the God who is present with us for our good, the God who loves us in multiple ways, wherever and however we may be? How do you open folk to the sense of God? How do you feed that hunger?

Your life will be bread for those who hunger for God. Your teaching others "I love you" in verbal and nonverbal ways will be food for the spirit. God's love is mediated most often through one another. You will be the bread of God in the world. And sometimes it will feel too much for you; sometimes you will be overwhelmed and say, "How can I be the bread of God for so many people?"

Especially in those times, return to the table of God. Take physical bread, bless it, break it, distribute it, eat it, and in the tangibility of that bread be reminded that you become the bread of God not through your own strength, but through God's strength, feeding your spirit. You will be renewed at this table in the community of God's people. There is strength enough, and more left over, for the work God calls you to do.

So eat one last time at this table in this community. Watch the bread multiply, taste it, swallow it. Gather up its fragments and take them to a hungry world. For this is the multiplication table of our Lord, where we learn to say in many languages and in all our living, "I love you."

City of God

Text: Hebrews 12:18–24

I live near the city of Los Angeles, in California, and often I have occasion to drive from Claremont into the city. The freeway takes me through the towns and then up a very steep incline known as Kellogg Hill. And at the very top of that hill, on a very clear day, suddenly there I see it: a city, rising from a plain that is itself ringed by the snowcapped San Gabriel mountains. From that spot on top of the hill the city indeed looks like the City of Angels. The buildings, clustered together, rise like wings from the plain, announcing that this is indeed Los Angeles, which in Spanish means the City of the Angels.

And when I come into the city, there are indeed wonderful sights to see. Amidst the buildings there are sparkling fountains and pools, and flowers blooming all the year round, and parks, and of course great buildings and museums. And it is a city of many cultures: Korea town, and Japan town, and China town, and south-Central, where many African-Americans live, and Alvera Street, where Mexican Americans show their culture. It is a city of many cultures come together in commerce and communication.

But this City of Angels is also a place of demons. There are drugs in this city, and places of homelessness and hopelessness. This is the city that all the world saw in 1992 as the city of riots, where African American and Korean American and Anglo American cultures clashed and burned and went up in flames. The City of Angels knows great poverty as well as great wealth, and all the problems of the world are present in some way or other in Los Angeles.

Preached at Yonsei University Chapel, Seoul, Korea.

111

Now I am in another great city of the world: Seoul. When I came for the first time to this city in 1994, I arrived at night. As I was driven from Kimpo airport into the city, I was first struck by the sign of the cross. For everywhere I looked I could see a cross in red neon marking the places of the many churches, so that my first experience was that I had come to the city of the sign of the cross. And in the daylight I visited some of these great churches and was shown as well the wonders of this city. I have seen the great National Treasure gate, wondering at its color and grace. And I have been taken to the Seoul tower and marveled at the beauty of this city seen from that height. I was taken to the sculpture gardens at the Shilla Hotel, and I have explored interesting streets and wonderful restaurants and marveled at dancing and drumming and other wonders bespeaking the beauty of Korean culture in this city of the sign of the cross.

But another scene I encountered was a bit more grim. I saw police dressed in black, getting off a bus that was barred like a prison. And I watched the police march two-by-two, riot shields held in their hands, and I knew that as in my own city of angels, all is not always well in this city of the sign of the cross. Here, as in my country, there is disheartenment over corruption and scandal in high places. And I shall never forget the day when my guide, driving me through the city, pointed to a spot on the sidewalk saying, "There is where my classmate from Yonsei was shot down and died during a student protest." This city of the sign of the cross is not always a sign of redemption, but is also a sign of deep suffering.

So what of our two cities, and how shall we view them in light of today's text? For the text says that there is yet another city, a city toward which we all journey: the city of the living God. What is this city? And what is its sign? And what does it have to do with Los Angeles and Seoul?

We are told in the book of Hebrews that the city of God is a place where God is judge, and where the spirits of the righteous are made perfect. If we turn to the Psalms, we read still more about this city. In Psalm 46, "There is a river whose streams make glad the city of God, the holy habitation of the

Most High." And the prophet Amos tells us that this river is a river of righteousness: "Let justice roll down like waters and righteousness like an ever-flowing stream" (Amos 5:24). And again the Psalms tell us something of this righteousness that is like water and an ever-flowing stream: "The Lord keeps faith forever, and executes justice for the oppressed, and gives food to the hungry. The Lord sets the prisoners free, the Lord opens the eyes of the blind. The Lord lifts up those who are bowed down; the Lord loves the righteous. The Lord watches over the strangers, and upholds the orphan and the widow" (Ps. 146:6–9, NRSV alt.).

So the city of God is a place where there are no culture wars; where there is no homelessness; where there is redress from oppression; where righteousness is made perfect. And I think that we who live in our cities of angels and crosses are so to live in our earthly cities that we judge them by that heavenly city. We are to live as citizens of two worlds, bringing the care and justice of God's city into these cities of ours. Heavenly eyes should guide our earthly seeing, so that we live God's justice here and now. We are to care for the widow and the orphan, for the stranger. We are to bring justice to the oppressed, provide food for the hungry, and with this justice we are to be a hope for these cities.

Throughout Christian history, the church has connected our longing for that heavenly city with responsible living in our earthly cities. Augustine saw the church as those whose love for God governed their actions in this world; Christians, he said, are citizens of the City of God. The great theologian Thomas Aquinas saw us as journeying ever toward a homeland, which is the perfect vision of God and therefore the City of God. Many persons in the Reformation understood the call of God to be for the creation of an earthly city that would mirror the heavenly city, and in our own century Walter Rauschenbusch made the City of God—or Kingdom of God—the criterion of all Christian theology and Christian living.

For all, the city of God is an ever-present hope within us that God's own justice is final, judging our earthly cities with the norm of care, compassion, and an openness that values the cultures of this world and yet transcends the cultures of this world. It is a justice that applies to every culture, a norm that measures every city. And we are called by God to let this justice and this norm guide our own actions in these earthly cities.

You are people with the future ahead of you. Will you live in these earthly cities of ours as ones who dare to bring the righteousness of God with you? Will you dare to let that stream of righteousness that makes glad the City of God flow through you? Will you as citizens of God's city be a blessing of justice to this earthly city? The future is before you: God's future is before you. And you have the opportunity so to open your own lives to God's justice that through you God will yet bring justice, righteousness, peace to the earthly city. And when you dare to choose to do this, then God's own hope hovers over our cities. They may yet indeed be touched by an angel, redeemed by a cross.

Amen.

Rekindle the Gift

Text: 2 Timothy 1:1–14

Listen for story within the text. The first generation of Christians were passing away, for Lois first had faith, then her daughter, and now Paul is addressing a third-generation Christian, the grandson and son who was Timothy. The family had known Paul for a long time, and it had been Paul himself who had given Timothy the laying on of hands. By now Timothy was probably a mid- to late teenager. Paul had been his ideal, his hero, one particularly marked by the grace of God who had been throughout the world preaching Christ. And perhaps to Timothy nothing bad could ever happen to Paul; he was such a good Christian that surely God would take care of him and protect him.

But now Paul is writing this letter from prison, and it is serious. It is a dangerous time, for the emperor is cruelly crushing the Christian movement, putting to death those who refuse to bow to Caesar. The implication of the text is that Timothy is not only afraid, he is ashamed of the gospel. He has prayed for Paul, he has trusted God to protect him, but what good has it done! Now Paul is imprisoned, and in terrible danger of being put to death! Where is God in this tragedy? Of what good is the gospel, if it cannot protect its finest people?

I can identify with the text. I am a grandmother, a woman of faith, as is my daughter Catherine. And Garth is Catherine's son, my grandson, and he is mad at God. His dad, Catherine's husband and my son-in-law Butch, had been diagnosed with leukemia. Butch was a Christian, and had taught his little son how to pray, and so Garth prayed for his dad, as did the whole family and, indeed, the whole

---

Delivered at First United Methodist Church, Tucson, Arizona.

congregation of their little church. Surely, since his dad was such a good Christian, and with so many people praying for him, Butch would recover from this dreadful disease! Surely he would not die!

But Butch did die, in the midst of a bone marrow transplant that came too late. Butch died, and his eight-year-old Garth played "Jesus Loves Me" on his violin during the funeral. Jesus loves me! What kind of love is this, that doesn't protect my dad? And so while Garth continues to go to church with his mother—and with his grandmother, too, when she is in town—I've noticed that he doesn't really participate. He doesn't sing the hymns, or say the words of the liturgy, or add his own voice to the prayers. Cathy says, "He's mad at God."

Is there a "Timothy" or "Garth" in your life? Do you know one whose faith is flickering, who is discouraged, disheartened, and doubting? Have you been "Timothy" or "Garth" at some point in your life? Turn with me back to the text, for perhaps Paul's words to his Timothy will be helpful to us.

The text gives us guidance not only by what Paul says, but by what Paul does. First, Paul recounts the stories. He tells the great story of the gospel: that God has called us from all eternity with a holy calling, that God's purposes and grace have been revealed to us in Christ Jesus, and that in Jesus death has been abolished, and life and immortality now shine in the gospel. In addition to the great story of the gospel, he intimates the smaller stories of his own life, and that of Timothy's family. It's as if Paul is saying to Timothy, Remember the stories. There are the stories of Paul's own life, such as we can read in second Corinthians, chapter 11; there are the stories of his grandmother's faith and his mother's faith— personal stories that belong especially to Timothy. And there are the larger stories that belong to us all, stories of God's work with the people of Israel and with the infant church. Remember the stories; tell the stories!

But in telling the stories, we must see that they give us no reason to believe that what God gives us as Christians is protection from all harm. There are no grounds in scripture to think that we, or those we love, will never become victims of leukemia, or AIDS, or crime, or accident, or harm from others. Christian faith is not an amulet; it does not protect us from terrible things happening.

What it does give us is the assurance that God's love surrounds us, is shared with us, and that our own love can be deepened so that we will find the strength not only to endure hardships, but to be transformed through them into persons who have grown deeper into compassion and love. We are not promised protection from danger; we are promised the power to endure all dangers without being destroyed in our very souls.

And what we learn through the stories is that the love of God is stronger than death. This life, this precious life, is caught up in the everlasting life of God, now and forever! Even when the worst of things happen, and bring us death—whether through beheading for the apostle Paul or through leukemia for my dear son-in-law—we dare to believe through Christ that we are a resurrection people! The very love of God that embraces us in this life embraces us forever, and with Christ we are raised into God's own resurrection life. God's love is stronger than death, and we are made participants in the eternal life of God.

But how do we say such things in a way that can be heard? How can little Garth learn to trust again, and let go his anger at God? Here we look to what Paul does. And we learn two things: He prays for Timothy night and day; and he loves Timothy thoroughly and deeply, regardless of the lad's struggles.

And we as the community of Christ are responsible for praying for one another during our hard times, and for loving one another faithfully during our deepest troubles. We are called to share our own stories, as well as the stories of scripture, all in the context of the Great Story, which is the gospel of our Lord and Savior Jesus Christ. In this loving and praying and sharing of stories, we may find that we might yet rekindle the gift of faith in our Timothys, our Garths, and ourselves. So may it be.

For finally the word of the gospel is not that we shall be protected from all harm, but that we shall be strengthened with all love, so that our exultant cry, even through our tears, is Romans 8: Who shall separate us from the love of God? Shall leukemia or any illness, shall the death of a father, or mother, or child, or spouse, shall accident or misfortune, shall alcoholism, or divorce, or loneliness, or nakedness, or peril, or sword?...In all these things we overwhelmingly conquer through him who loved us. For I am convinced that neither death, nor life, nor angels, nor principalities, nor things present, nor things to come, nor powers, nor height, nor depth, nor any other created thing, shall be able to separate us from the love of God, which is in Christ Jesus our Lord. Amen.

Notes

[1]The story, of course, comes from *City of God*, Books 11 and 12.

[2]John Wesley, *A Plain Account of Christian Perfection* (London: Epworth Press, 1952).

[3]Ibid., 86–88.

[4]Kathy Black, *A Healing Homiletic: Preaching and Disabilities* (Nashville: Abingdon Press, 1996).

[5]See Walter Rauschenbusch, *A Theology for the Social Gospel* (New York: Macmillan, 1917).

[6]See John B. Cobb, Jr., *Christ in a Pluralistic Age* (Philadelphia:Westminster, 1975).

[7]Paul G. Hewitt, *Conceptual Physics*, 8th ed. (Reading, Mass.: Addison-Wesley, 1998), 181.

[8]Ibid.